MW00629226

CHRONICLES OF
HISTORY
AND
WORSHIP

Orthodox Christian Reflections on
the Books of Chronicles

by Patrick Henry Reardon

Conciliar Press
Ben Lomond, California

CHRONICLES OF HISTORY AND WORSHIP:
Orthodox Christian Reflections on the Books of Chronicles
© Copyright 2006 by Patrick Henry Reardon

All Rights Reserved

Published by   Conciliar Press
                    P.O. Box 76
                    Ben Lomond, California 95005-0076

Printed in the United States of America

ISBN 10: 1-888212-83-7
ISBN 13: 978-1-888212-83-9

in loving memory of
Lynette

CONTENTS

INTRODUCTION

۶

IF IT IS THE CASE—AND LIKELY IT IS—that the Books of Chronicles are among the most neglected parts of the Bible, the loss is surely to those who do the neglecting. Indeed, I confess to having suffered that loss for many years. I had read Chronicles regularly, of course, as a simple matter of duty, but with scant understanding of what I read. I had no adequate guide to introduce and direct my study of this important biblical theologian. Only in old age have I come to grasp and appreciate the quiet, contemplative perception of biblical history found in Chronicles, which I now regard as among the most theologically mature books of the Hebrew Bible.

My own relative neglect for many years, however, prompts a sense of compassion for those other readers who find the Books of Chronicles rough going. It is a fact that the work of the Chronicler is not easy for beginners, for whom the present commentary is intended as a modest introduction and guide. I so hope my effort will meet this need, because the informed reader will find in Chronicles a robust diet for the spirit.

With respect to these books, however, the number of readers that can be called "beginners" may be rather large. Indeed, many brave souls, summoning their inner resources and mounting an effort to the task, have found even the opening chapter daunting.

For one thing, nothing much seems to be happening. In the Hebrew and Greek texts, in fact, the Chronicler does not get around to his first verb ("begot," naturally) until verse 10. Before that mildly exciting moment, the first page of Chronicles is a bare list of names.

The beginning reader, looking for a plot in the story, is disconcerted. Aware that the page in front of him is the Word of God, he is understandably hesitant to call it boring. Nonetheless, what is he to make of all these interminable names with no discernible narrative? He finds himself plodding through a primitive phone book, as it were, published long before the telephone was invented. This view would at least explain why the numbers are missing.

Most readers, after all, are prone to associate good storytelling with at least an occasional recourse to verbs. Verbs make things *happen*, and if nothing happens, there isn't much of a story. This, I suppose, is an assumption we picked up early. For example, among our very first literary adventures there was "See Spot run," a sound, robust imperative with a hearty ratio of two verbs to one noun. This is lean, muscular literature that seldom gets livelier. Perhaps our expectations of literary excitement were unduly raised by that enduring vision of Spot on the run.

By any standard, nonetheless, the first chapter of the Chronicler is extraordinarily short on verbs. "Begot" appears six times, and "reigned" twice or so. That just about does it. Well, the verb "died" does come seven times toward the end of the chapter, but by then the reader may feel like doing the same.

Moreover, the problem is not confined to the first chapter. If the reader gets this far, he must still trek through another eight chapters before he arrives, as though with a trumpet fanfare, at that glorious oasis opening on chapter 10: "Now the Philistines fought against Israel; and the men of Israel fled from before the Philistines, and fell slain on Mount Gilboa." Aha, he says to himself, some real action at last. Spot is finally on the run.

He quickly discovers, nonetheless, that chapter 10 has only fourteen verses, and most of the next two chapters go right back to more lists of names. Perhaps by the time he reaches chapter 21 the reader is completely in sympathy with the Lord's punishment of David for taking a census!

To gain some perspective on this dilemma, I think it useful to recall the Greek name for the Books of Chronicles, *Paralipomena*, which means "stuff left out." Although this name does not do justice to the Chronicler's intention, it does indicate what he did *not* intend to do. He did *not* intend to give us the whole story. Consequently, the Chronicler omitted a great deal. Indeed, at many points (all of chapter 1, for instance) he manifestly presumed his readers already knew the story.

The Chronicler's intention was, rather, to tell the story from a perspective different from those of the other biblical historians. Like the authors of Genesis, Samuel, and Kings, the Chronicler had in mind to grasp the meaning of Israel's history, not simply to relate the facts, and readers owe him the responding effort to discern what he thought that historical meaning to be. Because of the difficulties already noted, this effort may have to be considerable, and it is true that relatively few Christian readers have bothered with it.

In fact, many readers of Chronicles, perhaps overly impressed by the Greek title in use among Christians until fairly recent times, have treated these books as merely *paralipomena*, just "stuff left out" of the racier, more exciting, See-Spot-run pages of Samuel and Kings. The work of the Chronicler is often pursued as though it offered only a dull supplement to these other books.

In the standard Hebrew text, indeed, this impression is strengthened by the Chronicler's place at the very end of the Bible, where the final editors of the Masoretic text inappropriately set it. The Greek Bible, in contrast, at least has the merit of putting the Books of Chronicles in front of Ezra and Nehemiah, which are the proper continuation of the Chronicler's narrative.

Unless the reader grasps the Chronicler's historical perspective and literary intention, these books will continue to be obscure. It was to address that need that the present commentary was written.

Let the reader of the present work be resolved, then, to read it *as an aid* to the study of the Books of Chronicles, *not* as a substitute for that study. It is the present author's intention to *help* the reading of the Bible, not to distract from it or replace it. (I can hardly describe my horror when some folks mentioned reading *Christ in the Psalms* in place of the Book of Psalms!)

The Mind of the Chronicler

Who, then, was the Chronicler, and what did he have in mind to say? It is not possible to identify the Chronicler with assurance, nor to pin down with certainty the date of his work. Some historians, taking their cue from the Talmud (*Baba Bathra* 15a), identify him as the great Ezra, but these same scholars also disagree—by as much as sixty years—about the date of Ezra's mission.

However, I do not think the reasons for identifying the Chronicler as Ezra himself, or even as the author of Ezra-Nehemiah, are convincing, nor do they explain why some of the dominant theological and liturgical themes in the Books of Chronicles are largely absent in the pages of Ezra-Nehemiah. I am disposed to say that there appears to be *some* sort of literary relationship between Ezra-Nehemiah and the Books of Chronicles, and leave it at that.

So when did the Chronicler write? If it is implausible—and a consensus says it is—to place him earlier than the mid-fifth century, when Nehemiah arrived in Jerusalem, the earliest possible time of composition would be the late fifth or early fourth century.

What, then, is the latest possible time of the Chronicler's work? Inasmuch as the priestly genealogy in 1 Chronicles 3:19–24 seems to extend to six generations after Zerubbabel in the late sixth century, we will not be much off if we suggest some date close to 400 BC. Thus, it is reasonable to think that the Chronicler wrote during the second half of the Persian period, before the rise of Alexander and its ensuing trauma. This loose dating is sufficient to help the reader understand what the Chronicler had in mind to say.

After the edict of Cyrus in 538, the exiles returning from Babylon carried many questions in their minds. One of these questions had to do with the covenant promises made to the house of David. The Davidic monarchy had been abolished, and although some still hoped for its eventual restoration, that restoration did not seem likely—certainly not while the Persians held sway.

The Persian Empire, the new power in the Fertile Crescent, did not intend to encourage underling kings, an institution tolerated by the Assyrians and Babylonians who preceded them. Persian rule would be structured on geographical districts known as satrapies, with all satraps and other officials appointed by the emperor. Thus, when Cyrus assigned Zerubbabel to oversee the return of the Jewish exiles in 538, this royal descendant of David did not come to Jerusalem as a king but only as an appointed governor.

Moreover, the Persians had no intention to leave Zerubbabel in Judah very long after the initial settling of the returning exiles. Indeed, given the messianic aspirations to be found among some of these latter (cf. Hag. 2:21–22; Zech. 4:6–7), it would be too risky for the Persians to leave a son of David in charge at Jerusalem. It is not clear when Zerubbabel returned to Babylon, but we observe that his name is not found among those present at the new temple's completion in 515 (Ezra 6:14), nor is there any record of another governor from the Davidic family appointed to Jerusalem.

As time went on, then, and the citizens of Judah became ever more accustomed to living under Persian rule and without a Davidic king, those given to reflection on their history were obliged to think anew on the meaning of the house of David. In view of the obvious fact that the covenanted monarchy at Jerusalem was now gone, what was to be made of the divine promise that David's throne would last forever? In the light of all the recent events, what was to be said about the monarchical house of the son of Jesse? What was the true historical significance of that institution?

These questions were pondered deeply by thoughtful minds, both during the Babylonian Exile (cf. Ezek. 34:23–24; 37:24–25) and during the ensuing years (cf. the late-sixth-century editor of Is. 55:3–5 and the still later hand in Zech. 12:8–10). Also numbered among those who pondered these questions in depth was the Chronicler.

In respect to David's royal house, any Bible-reader can see how profoundly the Chronicler's perspective differed from the historical interest in Samuel–Kings, a narrative finished much earlier, probably during the Babylonian Captivity. Although the author of Samuel–Kings had a great deal to say of the house of David, it is clear his historical interest was much broader. He does not appear to be arguing some thesis dominated by the Davidic monarchy.

An examination of the work makes this clear. Recording the two centuries during which the kingdoms of Israel and Judah co-existed (922–722), the Books of Kings (or "Kingdoms," as they are known in the Septuagint) devoted more space to the schismatic Kingdom of Israel than to the covenanted monarchy of Judah. In Kings we learn more about Jeroboam than about Rehoboam, far more about Ahab than about Jehoshaphat. It is obvious, then, that the complex of Samuel–Kings is not built around the Davidic covenant and throne as a thematic center.

When we turn to the Books of Chronicles, on the other hand, the significance of the Davidic throne is impossible to exaggerate. For all practical purposes, the Northern Kingdom does not even exist! This author mentions that schismatic nation only when he absolutely must. In Chronicles the very name "Samaria" is found only eight times, and always in connection with wars against Judah. Clearly the author would rather not mention the Northern Kingdom at all. His interest has entirely to do, rather, with Judah and Jerusalem, and his mind is engrossed with one question: "What was the real and lasting significance of David and his house?"

The True Significance of David's House

Of the 65 chapters contained in the Books of Chronicles, 19 are devoted to the reign of King David (1 Chr. 11—29). This bare fact sufficiently indicates the importance of David in the mind of the Chronicler.

But even more significant, I believe, are the concerns the Chronicler decided to treat within these 19 chapters and the way he proportioned those concerns in the narrative. Of these 19 chapters devoted to David, the Chronicler allotted no fewer than 11—over half—to describe that king's solicitude for Israel's proper worship (1 Chr. 13; 15—16 and 22—29). This material includes the transfer of the ark of the covenant to Jerusalem, the organization of the priestly and Levitical ministries, preparations for the sacred music, and David's lengthy instructions to Solomon with respect to the temple.

According to the Chronicler, David not only made all the arrangements for the construction of the temple and the organization of the worship (1 Chr. 28:19), he did so by the Lord's own command (2 Chr. 29:25). Even the musical instruments used in the worship are credited to David (2 Chr. 29:27; cf. Neh. 12:36).

To grasp the significance of this liturgical emphasis of the Chronicler, it is useful to compare his account of David's reign to that in the Books of Samuel. In Samuel there are 77 verses devoted to David's liturgical interests, whereas in the Chronicles there are 323. According to the Chronicler, that is to say, David's major importance as an historical figure had to do with his efforts with respect to the divine worship. It was precisely David's work for the temple and its liturgy that rendered him most significant in the history of the people of God.

As the Chronicler could plainly see from looking around him, surveying the circumstances of his own life and times, David's one enduring accomplishment was his singular, unparalleled contribution to Israel's worship. Everything else about David had disappeared from the earth. His battles and conquests were only faint memories. Other details of David's life (his adultery and murder, certainly) were best forgotten. His hereditary throne had disappeared, like all the other thrones of history. For this reason also, the Chronicler omits all discussion of David's life prior to his becoming king. This otherwise interesting material was simply not pertinent to his theme.

By the Chronicler's time, the only thing left that made David a truly important historical figure was the body of his achievements on behalf of Israel's authentic and proper worship of God. David's liturgical accomplishments alone had survived the ravages of history, but for the author of Chronicles these achievements were quite enough, and his long historical reflection was based on them.

Following this conviction about David's true place in history, the Chronicler went on to regard the rest of Judah's kings through that same lens. Of the nine chapters he devoted to the reign of Solomon, the Chronicler used six to tell of the building, appointing, and dedicating of the temple. After all, none of Solomon's other accomplishments had endured. Only his provision for Israel's worship made him a figure of historical consequence.

This theme of the royal patronage of Israel's worship continues through the remainder of the Chronicler's narrative. He alone tells us of the northern Levites who fled to Jerusalem to serve in the temple during the reign of Rehoboam (2 Chr. 11:13–17). Solely from the Chronicler do we learn of Asa's liturgical reforms (15:8–15), Jehoshaphat's sponsorship of the teaching Levites (17:7–9), and his prayer in the temple (20:5–12). Only the Chronicler condemns King Uzziah's interference with the priestly ministry of the temple (26:16–23). He alone describes in detail certain liturgical reforms of Hezekiah (29:12—31:21), Manasseh (33:15–17), and Josiah (35:2–18).

When the Chronicler speaks, then, of "the mercies of David" (*hasde Dawid*—6:42; cf. Ps. 89[88]:2, 3, 50; Is. 55:3), this expression has specific reference to Israel's worship, especially the liturgy in the temple. Although David's royal house had not been restored to the throne, the Lord's own house, the temple, had been rebuilt since the return from exile, and even now it served as the place of His authentic and orthodox worship.

In the Chronicler's time, the final fortunes of the Davidic royal family were still unknown, but this author was yet able to point to its one undeniable historical achievement. David's line had fashioned and equipped Israel's true worship. That was their contribution to sacred history.

Remembering David

The historical perspective of the Chronicler was perhaps most poetically expressed in one of the final "Psalms of Ascent," those hymns chanted by the pilgrims to Jerusalem as they climbed the hill on their way to the temple. This psalm, Psalm 132 (Greek and Latin 131), prays the Lord to "remember David / And all his afflictions," those things he suffered to establish the service of the temple. It goes on to associate closely the fortunes of the Davidic house with the blessings of the house of the Lord. The psalmist believes that if the Lord really *remembers* David, He will clothe Zion's priests with salvation and cause her saints to sing for joy. All these things are done *in remembrance of David.* In this entire psalm there is not one word of anything else David accomplished except his provision for the temple's worship.

If it is thus that Israel prays the Lord to remember David, it is because this is how the Lord's people themselves should remember David, especially as they tread those final uphill steps to enter the Lord's courts with praise and thanksgiving. David was the founder of it all. Because of God's promise to David, a special protection attended His temple and the worship that took place in that temple. This psalm guaranteed that Israel would not enter the house of the Lord without thinking on the king who saw to its construction and provision.

This is exactly how the Chronicler too remembered David—as the true builder of Solomon's temple, the spiritual leader who arranged its priestly and Levitical ministries, the master liturgist who composed its music and provided the singers and instruments to give it voice. Compared with these accomplishments, little else about David was worth remembering.

Moreover, and more importantly, the Chronicler's view of David is inseparable from his view of Israel. For the Chronicler, what made David different from all other kings of the earth is exactly what made Israel different from all other nations of the earth—the knowledge and correct worship of the one true God.

David did not inaugurate Israel's worship, of course. That task was given to Moses and his brother Aaron, and if the Chronicler seems to neglect that earlier part of Israel's liturgical history, it is because he knew that story had already been told and was readily available. In the books of Exodus, Leviticus, and Numbers, the Chronicler recognized the earlier proper treatment of his own chosen theme, and it was his intention to carry that Mosaic story on to its later stages, especially as embodied in the liturgy of the temple.

It is in this theme of orthodox worship that we perceive the historical perspective of the Chronicler. To his mind, the deepest and most enduring fact of history is the correct, covenanted worship of the true God by His chosen people. Beside this, everything else is relatively insignificant. For him, all other aspects of man's history are judged in importance by their relationship to this standard, for in the estimation of the Chronicler only the correct worship of the true God gives lasting significance to the deeds of men. This is the guiding principle manifest throughout all the narrative we are considering.

At least one other biblical theologian shared the Chronicler's conviction about the relationship between history and worship, because more than two centuries later we find the same perspective in the Son of Sirach. "Let us now praise famous men," that wise man solemnly begins, "and our fathers that begot us" (Ecclus. 44:1), and then he goes on to trace the high points of biblical history in the characters of Enoch, Noah, Abraham and the other patriarchs, Moses, Joshua, Caleb, Samuel, David and Solomon, Elijah, Hezekiah, Isaiah, Josiah, Jeremiah, Ezekiel, Zerubbabel, and Nehemiah.

But what, for Ben Sirach, constituted the crowning and glorious achievement of all this lengthy history? The worship in the temple, which he describes in stirring detail in chapter 50. Here we see him relishing the grandeur and beauty of the temple liturgy, presided over by Simon the high priest, as the sons of Aaron chant the praises of God and all the worshippers prostrate themselves in adoration. Israel's history finds its culmination, fulfillment, and meaning in its worship.

Earlier in the same narrative, moreover, Ben Sirach prepares his readers for that grand scene in the temple by describing David's provision for this worship in the arrangement of liturgical feasts and seasons, the composition of hymns, and the establishing of choirs to sing them (Ecclus. 47:8–10). Ben Sirach's view of history and worship, then, seems identical to that of the Chronicler.

Levi and Judah

In spite of the Chronicler's dominating interest in David, and notwithstanding the basing of his narrative structure on the sequence of the Davidic kings, the theological perspective in the Books of Chronicles is not that of the royal tribe of Judah. The writer is not simply a traditional apologist of the Davidic throne.

To virtually all Bible-readers it is obvious that the Chronicler crafts his history, rather, from the perspective of a minister of the temple. His viewpoint may be described as more clerical than royal, hierarchical rather than monarchical. Thus, he has vastly more to say about the ministry of the temple than about the other concerns of the king's palace.

In fact, we may describe the Chronicler's perspective even more precisely. He writes, not simply as a minister of the temple, but specifically as a Levite, this term meaning a male member of the house of Levi who is *not* a descendant of Aaron. This would explain the Chronicler's truly singular interest in the Levitical ministries of the temple.

A simple word count will demonstrate this interest. The term "Levite," which is found only five times, and in only one chapter, of the Book of Leviticus, appears in Chronicles ninety-nine times. If we add in the instances of "Levites" in Ezra-Nehemiah, we come to a total of 158 times, more than in all the other books of the Bible combined. Moreover, it is the Chronicler alone who provides such detailed genealogies of the various Levitical families, including the sort of information normally associated with family records.

These Levites not only assisted the priests, the sons of Aaron, in the preparation of the sacrifices, they also cared for other aspects of the temple. Some served as doorkeepers, for instance, some as singers and musicians, and, at certain periods of history, some served as teachers of the Law. The Chronicler shows a pointed interest in all these ministries.

Can we further narrow the focus of the Chronicler? Perhaps we can. Among the various ministries the Levites performed in the prescribed worship, the Chronicler reveals a particular regard for the liturgical music.

This regard is manifest if we simply compare the Chronicler's stories with those in Kings, where the verb "to sing," *shir*, is found only one time (1 Kings 10:12). For example, unlike the parallel account in 2 Kings 11, the Chronicler tells of the activity of the temple singers and musicians in the deposition of the usurper Athaliah (2 Chr. 23:13). Again, the Chronicler alone speaks of the music sung and played during the transference of the ark to the newly constructed temple (2 Chr. 5:12–13). More than one reader, impressed by this evidence, has found it easy to believe that the Chronicler sprang from one of the "singing families" among the Levites, perhaps the house of Asaph, whom David placed over the temple's musical ministries and whose name appears so frequently in the titles of various psalms.

Without pressing the case further, we may at least conclude that the Chronicler represents the perspective of the ministerial tribe of Levi rather than the royal tribe of Judah. Furthermore, as we shall see in the commentary, he directs a great deal of his attention to the relationship between these two tribes.

The ministerial tribe of Levi was born of Jacob's third son, while the tribe of Judah was sired by his fourth. Furthermore, Israel had a hierarchy long before and long after it had a monarchy. Thus, from the very beginning the priesthood of Israel enjoyed an ascendancy of sorts over the royalty.

The relationship between these two Israelite tribes invites comparisons with similar examples from the history of religion. One thinks, for instance, of ancient India, where the *raja* (from the same root as the Latin *rex*, meaning "king") belonged to the ruling caste of the Kshatryas, the caste immediately *below* that of the priests, or Brahmins. Occasional religious frictions between the two groups, in fact, eventually spawned two new religions, when Mahavira and Siddartha Gautama, both of them from the Kshatryas caste, broke with the Brahmins and became the "founders" of Jainism and Buddhism, respectively. It is exceedingly curious that these things happened in the sixth century BC, about the time that Israel lost its monarchy but kept its priesthood.

In the Bible there is no socioreligious crisis comparable to that in Hinduism. With very few exceptions, such as Uzziah (2 Chr. 26:16–20), the kings of Judah did not encroach on the prerogatives of the clergy. In those instances where David or Solomon is said to offer sacrifice, it is said in much the same sense as saying that David or Solomon built a bridge or constructed a wall—that is to say, they caused the thing to be done. Nor, on the other hand, did Israel's priesthood attempt to usurp the duties and privileges of the throne. There is no reason to question the Chronicler's overall portrait of the two institutions working together in harmony.

As we shall see in the commentary, in fact, the temple's priesthood was effective in saving the Davidic throne in its hour of greatest danger—the six years during which the infidel daughter of Ahab and Jezebel replaced the sons of David. The story of the restoration of young Joash to the Davidic throne by the high priest Jehoiada (2 Chr. 23) is among the most memorable narratives in Holy Scripture.

Still, the Chronicler's perspective on these matters was that of the clergy, not the royalty. He evaluates the kings of Judah largely on the basis of their attention to and care for the worship. By that standard, such kings as David, Solomon, Hezekiah, and Josiah received very good marks. Some of the others did not, and perhaps the worst of them all turned out to be Joash, who "did not remember the kindness which Jehoiada his father had done to him, but killed his son" (2 Chr. 24:22).

Chronicles and Christology

Our reflection on this rapport between Israel's kings and her priests is perhaps the best point at which to consider a proper Christian reading of Chronicles. Christians believe, after all, that the concord and affirmation between hierarchy and monarchy, as affirmed in Chronicles, is rendered perfect in God's Word incarnate as both priest and king. We confess that in the person of Jesus the Lord, perfect priesthood and complete kingship are forever joined. We should further acknowledge that the unity in Christ of these two institutions serves as the standard and model for interpreting their history as narrated in Chronicles.

First, kingship. Jesus is everywhere in the New Testament confessed as Son of David and the proper, eternal heir to his throne. As such, the early Christians believed, Jesus is the fulfillment of the covenant promise made to David that his Son would forever rule over Israel: "He will be great, and will be called the Son of the Highest; and the Lord God will give Him the throne of His father David. And He will reign over the house of Jacob forever, and of His kingdom there will be no end" (Luke 1:32–33). This is a standard and ubiquitous understanding throughout the New Testament (e.g., Matt. 1:2–16; 22:42–45; Rom. 1:2–4; 2 Tim. 2:8).

Second, priesthood. Since there was attached to the priesthood of the Old Testament no explicit covenant entirely equivalent to the kingly covenant made with David, Christians needed a bit more reflection to arrive at an understanding of Jesus as priest. This they were able to do because they believed that on the cross the Savior offered Himself in sacrifice, specifically as a sin offering, the sacrifice of atonement. From the very beginning this fundamental soteriological thesis was transmitted regularly in the words pronounced at the center of Christian worship: "This is My blood of the new covenant, which is shed for many for the remission of sins" (Matt. 26:28).

St. Paul used the same liturgical category, the sin offering, with

respect to the cross when he preached, as a matter of primary importance, that "Christ died for our sins" (1 Cor. 15:3). He later returned to
this image of the sin offering in Colossians 1:14 and Ephesians 1:7,
using in both places the same words, "we have redemption through His
blood, the forgiveness of sins." In Ephesians 5:2 Paul used even more
explicit liturgical language to say, "Christ also has loved us and given
Himself for us, an offering and a sacrifice to God for a sweet-smelling
aroma."

But if Jesus offered sacrifice, these Christians reflected, then Jesus is
a priest. The conclusion was inevitable. Hence, it is not surprising to
find two New Testament writers identifying Jesus as a priest. These writers
are St. Luke and the anonymous author of the Epistle to the Hebrews.
It is further significant to our study of Chronicles that both writers refer
to Jesus' priesthood in the context of His kingship. We may look at
these two authors in turn.

We may start with Luke, whose identification of Jesus as priest is
studiously quiet and understated. First, Luke mentions, as though in
passing, that Jesus' Mother is kin (*syggenis*—1:36) to a "daughter of
Aaron" (1:5), a subtle suggestion, easily unnoticed, of Levitical blood in
Jesus Himself. Luke's delicate hint is apparently compatible with his
assertion that Jesus was a descendant of Judah (3:33).

Second, St. Ambrose draws attention to a literary *inclusio* formed
by Luke's two references to the throwing of dice, both in the context of
sacrifice. The first instance, which determines Zacharias's liturgical task
of offering incense in the temple (1:9), stands in correspondence to the
later throwing of dice at the foot of the cross, the altar where Jesus offers
Himself in the supreme sacrifice (23:34). Ambrose comments, "It was
read in the dice which priest should enter the temple. . . . What else was
signified but that there would come a Priest . . . who would not offer
sacrifice for us in the temple made with hands, but would annul [*vacuaret*]
our sins in the temple of His body? Perhaps on this account the soldiers
cast dice for the Lord's garments. As the Lord prepared to offer sacrifice
for us in His temple, the shaking of the dice before Him would also
fulfill the precept of the Law" (*In Lucam* 1.23).

We likewise observe in Luke's second instance of dice rolling that
Jesus offers His sacrifice under a sign identifying Him as the king (Luke
23:38), thus fulfilling the promise of royalty made at the beginning
(1:32–33). That inscription proclaiming His kingship was placed on

the cross by the same soldiers that rolled the dice at the foot of His altar. Luke's Gospel, then, joins the hierarchy and monarchy of Jesus in the sacrifice of the cross, where He is portrayed as the sacrificing king.

We may turn now to the Epistle to the Hebrews, which treats the priesthood and kingship of Jesus very differently from Luke. This author goes to considerable length to insist that our Lord's priesthood is of a completely different order from that of Aaron. To describe Jesus as both priest and king, he reverts to the Bible's earliest example of Melchizedek, who served "God Most High" as hierarch and monarch at Jerusalem, centuries before the sons of Judah and Levi took on those responsibilities (Gen. 14:18–20; Heb. 6:20—7:18). The priesthood of Jesus, prophesied in Psalm 109[110]:4, was to be "according to the order of Melchizedek" (Heb. 7:17), "in the likeness of Melchizedek" (7:15).

The priesthood of Jesus was not of the Levitical order, in which "every priest stands ministering daily and offering repeatedly the same sacrifices, which can never take away sins" (10:11). On the contrary, "our Lord arose from Judah, of which tribe Moses spoke nothing concerning priesthood" (7:14). His, then, is a royal priesthood, the priesthood of a king.

The author of Hebrews illustrates this union of priesthood and kingship in Jesus in a striking way: the priesthood of Jesus is perfected in His enthronement. The sacrifice offered by Jesus is rendered perfect by His entrance, once and for all, into the Holy Place not made by hands (9:11), in order "to appear in the presence of God for us" (9:24). This entrance into the heavenly sanctuary renders His sacrifice perfect, because "if He were on earth, He would not be a priest" (8:4).

But what did Jesus do when He entered the heavenly sanctuary? He did what no priest on earth would ever do in the earthly sanctuary. He sat down. He assumed His throne. It is a mark of priests on earth, says Hebrews, that they *stand* at the altar (10:11, *hesteken*). Not this Priest, however. This Priest is the King, who "when He had by Himself purged our sins, sat down at the right hand of the Majesty on high" (1:3). To Him we proclaim, "Your throne, O God, is forever and ever" (1:8; Ps. 44[45]:6). The same psalm that says, "You *are* a priest forever / According to the order of Melchizedek," also says, "Sit at My right hand" (Ps. 109[110]:1, 4; Heb. 1:13; 5:6, 7, 15; 8:1; 10:12; 12:2).

As the King, likewise, this Priest wears a crown (Heb. 2:7, 9). His is the royal priesthood, thus perfecting the concurrence of monarchy and hierarchy adumbrated in the Books of Chronicles.

A Christian Reading of Chronicles

I want to extend our consideration of a Christian study of the Chronicler by suggesting that there is more than one legitimate approach to the sacred text. Christian history itself testifies to this exegetical variety, in which the rich meaning of Holy Scripture is never reducible to just one framework nor to a single formula. The Church has always insisted that the Bible is open to more than one approach, as long as each interpreter stays within, and takes his guidance from, the Rule of Faith (as explained, for example, by St. Augustine of Hippo, *The City of God* 15.26).

We can start, for example, by mentioning the standard fourfold outline formulated by St. John Cassian in the early fifth century (*Conferences 14.8*).

This traditional outline speaks first of the literal or historical sense of the text, the meaning originally intended by the biblical writer himself. As applied to a Christian reading of Chronicles, the pursuit of this sense will endeavor to read the sacred text through the author's manifest theological and historical concerns and within the boundaries of the work's historical context. A great deal of the present commentary is devoted to this pursuit.

According to Cassian's outline, however, this literal sense of the Bible is transformed by its doctrinal significance discerned in the light of Christ. This is the deeper meaning of Holy Scripture indicated by the risen Lord, who "beginning at Moses and all the Prophets, expounded to them in all the Scriptures the things concerning Himself" (Luke 24:27).

Following the lead of St. Paul, sacred tradition calls this meaning the Bible's allegorical sense (*allegoroumena*—Gal. 4:24), the newer, more complete significance, the *sensus plenior* evoked from the sacred page through its fulfillment in the Mystery of Christ. Reading Chronicles according to this sense, the figure of David, for example, is perceived to be a *type* of Christ, who fulfills in a special, definitive way what that Old Testament prophet and king accomplished by way of allegory. Namely, Christ provides for God's people the true worship, the true priesthood, the true temple—all the things that David, through shadows and figures, provided in his own time.

The third sense in Cassian's traditional outline is the Bible's tropological or moral sense, its existential, practical, and concrete application to the life of the believing reader. We perceive this sense of the Old Testament in St. Paul's applications of the sacred text to the Christian's moral life, as when he wrote of the ancient Israelites in the desert, "all these things happened to them as examples, and they were written for our admonition, upon whom the ends of the ages have come" (1 Cor. 10:11). In addition to negative examples, such as the one cited by Paul, the New Testament offers many positive Old Testament models, such as Elijah (Jas. 5:17) and Rahab (Heb. 11:31).

The work of the Chronicler, approached in this tropological sense, is full of myriad moral examples, both positive and negative, applicable to the life of the Gospel. Thus, the Christian reader is inspired to emulate such models as the foresight of David, the integrity of Jotham, the loyalty of Jehoiada, the courage of Micaiah, and so on, while cautiously eschewing the folly of Rehoboam, the infidelity of Jehoram, the cruelty of Athaliah, the ingratitude of Joash, and so forth.

The Christian reader, in his assessment of these moral examples, will be careful to interpret the text, not only according to the ethical standards of the Old Testament, but also in the full light of the Gospel. That is to say, the Christian moral life is always life under the guidance of the Holy Spirit, not according to the bondage of the Law.

Still following Cassian's interpretive outline, the fourth level of significance in Holy Scripture—its anagogical or eschatological sense—is the meaning that it has with respect to the last things, the definitive fulfillment of all history. Interpreted in this sense, the Books of Chronicles present us with a prophetic adumbration of man's eternal destiny, his worship before the Throne of God in glory. Everything the Chronicler has to say with respect to priesthood, sacrifice, hymnography, and prayer is a preparation for the everlasting worship described in, say, the Epistle to the Hebrews (e.g., 12:18–24) and the Book of Revelation (e.g., 5:8–14).

Another Christian Approach

In addition to the fourfold exegetical pattern outlined by St. John Cassian, let me suggest another Christian avenue to the Old Testament, one with a particular application to the Books of Chronicles.

This second approach differs from Cassian's in the following way. Cassian's doctrinal outline is constructed on the actual process of the history of salvation. It begins with the history of the Old Testament in proper sequence, an understanding of the Hebrew Scriptures on their own terms, so to speak, their own meaning in their own settings, and then goes on to examine the Old Testament through the perspective of the New, the lens of Christ. This exegetical process is the movement from letter to spirit, in which the meaning of the New enhances the meaning of the Old Testament.

Next, there is the understanding of sacred Scriptures as they are read and applied in the concrete lives of Christians. Finally, there is the ultimate fulfillment of God's Word when all signs and images have been absorbed into the light of eternal beatitude. This progressive understanding of the Bible in four steps has a discerned chronology.

The approach I am suggesting does not proceed along that chronological path. It begins, not with the history of the Bible, but with the personal history of the Gentile (like myself) who comes to Christ, not through the inherited history of the Old Testament, but through the original, straightforward proclamation of the Gospel.

I ask myself, why should I be interested in those ancient Hebrew writings in the first place? What connection do they have with me? And I answer, those ancient books have no special connection with me except on account of Christ. Christ alone is my link to those writings. That is to say, I don't begin with the Old Testament. I begin with Christ. I commence with the Center. Christ is not only the Mediator between God and man; He is also the Mediator between the Old Testament and the Church. Except for Christ, why should the Church be theologically interested in the Old Testament?

In this way we Christians actually *begin* to grasp the Old Testament according to its spiritual meaning, its allegorical sense, its Christological significance. As Christians we only go to the Old Testament because it pertains to Jesus. Otherwise the Old Testament is, for us non-Jews, just another ancient book. We accept it as *our* Bible only because it is *Jesus'* Bible. In truth and strictly speaking, after all, it is only Christ that makes the Old Testament theologically pertinent to us. Without Christ, the Old Testament is not really *our* history. We have no continuity with it—it is not part of *our* memory—except through Christ.

The Christ that is proclaimed brings the Old Testament with Him in the proclamation. Indeed, the barest preaching of the Gospel includes the Old Testament, in the sense that what Jesus accomplished for our redemption was "according to the Scriptures" (1 Cor. 15:1–4). The Christ we proclaim is proclaimed *as* the fulfillment of the Scriptures. It is in these swaddling clothes that the Messiah is adorned.

Our Spirit-prompted acceptance of the Gospel, then, the saving gift of our faith by which we are joined to Christ, also joins us, through Christ, to the ancient faith of the Hebrews who awaited His coming. Through Christ, their history becomes our history; we are engrafted into the Bible's ongoing chronology. The Hebrew Scriptures become our own family album. The history of the Bible and the history of the Church form a single narrative, of which our lives are an integral part.

Let us apply this truth to the Books of Chronicles. I would like to do this by a series of affirmations.

First, that apparently uninteresting, taxing list of names with which the Chronicler begins has in Christ become our own family tree. Because of Christ, we are part of a single story. An earlier part of our story is narrated in the Books of Chronicles.

Second, like any family history, the story in Chronicles is selective and told with a distinct purpose. As we have already reflected, that purpose has to do with the understanding that worship is what finally gives meaning to history.

Third, this thesis from Chronicles is true of our own history. The chief task of the Church, on earth as it is in heaven, is the glorification of God according to the prescribed orthodox worship. This is a major lesson the Church is to learn from the Chronicler. Applied more particularly to our personal lives, Chronicles would have us affirm that the life pleasing to God is the life centered on the orthodox worship God has revealed to the world in the family history of His people. Everything else in history will disappear. All that remains will be the entirely correct and everlasting worship of God.

Fourth, Israel's ancient temptation to forget this truth is what chiefly brought about the series of disasters narrated in Chronicles. That story, too, is told for our learning, to preserve us from the same lack of discernment, lest we lose our way and become likewise reprobate.

History and Biblical Understanding

Inasmuch as the Books of Chronicles appear in the Bible as "historical books," it will be instructive, I believe, to say something about the relationship between history and Holy Scripture.

First, the Bible not only records history; it also creates history. By this I mean that the Bible, as written down, read, and proclaimed in the ongoing community of faith (the Church of both Testaments), influences and directs the course of history. We ourselves are part of the history created by Holy Scripture. We are the *qahal,* the *ecclesia,* the gathering of those who in the Holy Spirit are assembled to attend to God's Word. In the history it records, the Bible itself prolongs that history in those who receive it in faith.

Second, this unified history, comprised of what the Bible records and what the Bible creates, is a single, living, ongoing reality, in which there is a continuity between the words of Holy Scripture and the Church's understanding of those words. If there were to be a break between the Bible and its interpretation, that continuity would be lost. There would be a disruption in salvation history. This is the tragedy known as "heresy."

Third, this continuity is called Holy Tradition, which embraces, as a single reality, the history narrated in the Holy Scriptures, the Holy Scriptures themselves, and the one, holy, catholic, and apostolic Church that reads these Scriptures in her worship, understands them in her teaching, and proclaims them in her ministry to the world. The biblical history narrated in the Church by the reading and proclamation of the Scriptures is the early part of the Church's own history. It is *our* history, and we in the Church understand it as our history.

Fourth, the correct understanding of Holy Scripture includes what some of the Church Fathers (for instance, Didymus the Blind, *Job* 9.13; Isidore of Pelusium, *Letters* 4.203) called *theoria,* meaning the spiritual discernment of the inner meaning of the Bible through the lens of Christ.

This inner sense of Scripture is not abstract; it pertains to one's personal life in Christ as a living member of the Church. That is to say, true theoria involves understanding the Bible in such a way as to cast light on the actual living of the Christian life *in* the Church. The Bible becomes the mirror in which we see our true faces (Jas. 1:23). Theoria is not only an understanding of the Bible, but also an understanding of ourselves in relation to God. It entails the reading of the Bible as a path of self-knowledge and growth in the Holy Spirit.

Theoria includes the perception of historical analogies between our own lives and the history recorded in God's Word. What in the Bible is called theoria is in our souls called the image of God. Through the contemplation of these analogies, we understand our own life and grasp both what God is doing in those lives and also what we ourselves are supposed to do. This is a Spirit-given insight into the Word of God, permitting that Word to take the measure of our own existence.

Within the Rule of Faith handed down in the Holy Tradition of the Church, these spiritual insights into Holy Scripture are potentially infinite—*sed theoriae quasi infinitae*, as St. Bonaventure expressed it (*In Hexaemeron* 15.10). In these perceptions the past of the Bible is rendered effective in the life of the Christian, because both are parts of a single history. Through these theoriai the Holy Scriptures provide the pattern for understanding all of history. There can be no "theology of history" except through the full, experienced understanding of the Bible.

This spiritual exegesis of the sacred Scriptures, however, always takes place *in* history and pertains to the movement of history. The Bible is not a reservoir of truths that can be removed from an historical shape. Understanding of the Bible must not become something abstracted from the historical movement of the Bible itself. Its continuous line, which records history, is recorded within history and gives form and shape to future history.

What, then, should be said about dogmatic pronouncements by which the Church seems to "fix" doctrine, to remove biblical teaching from its historical context? The correct answer to this question, I believe, must involve two considerations.

First, such dogmatic pronouncements, far from being an abstraction from history, also take place *within* history. To solidify a doctrine into a dogma does not sunder the doctrine from history. History is not to be described solely as fluid. It is obvious that a great deal of history—the past!—is absolutely settled and fixed.

There is no history without continuity, and dogma is the guarantor of continuity. In this sense, dogma is essential to history. Dogmas are not timeless, but they are fixed and unchanging. Theology grows, but dogma does not develop. It is fixed, absolute, and dependable, giving guidance to subsequent history. I presume to cite, on this point, one of the most learned theologians of recent years: "Dogma is by no means a *new* Revelation. Dogma is only a witness. The whole meaning of dogmatic definition consists of testifying to unchanging truth, truth which was revealed and has been preserved from the beginning" (Georges Florovsky, *Collected Works*, Vol. 3, p. 30).

Second, such dogmatic pronouncements, even when they are formulated in a positive way (such as the *homoousios* of Nicaea), tend essentially to serve a negative purpose. To the extent that the fullness of revelation has already taken place in God's incarnate Word, there can be no new dogmas, only new heresies. Consequently, the dogmatic formulations of the Church are radically apophatic. They are "definitions" in the sense of setting limits (*fines*), lines to exclude heresy. They do not "clarify" divine revelation by adding light, as it were, to what is already the fullness of light.

Finally, there can be no real understanding of the Bible in the present without an understanding of the Bible in the past, both the past as recorded in the Bible itself and the past in the sense of the Church's historical understanding of the sacred text. The attempt to come to Holy Scripture outside of that long historical context is not only presumptuous; it also separates the reader from the Bible's own history. Again in the words of St. Bonaventure, "the knowledge of future things depends on the knowledge of past things" (*In Hexaemeron* 2.17). This can be hard work, but in the study of the Bible there is no substitute for the knowledge of history.

Accordingly, in the present commentary on the Books of Chronicles, this interpreter's first and dominating intention will be to place the sacred text in its historical setting, pointing out from time to time, as opportunity allows, how the Church has understood the message of these books.

But this is not only history, because the Chronicler was not only an historian but also a theologian of history. For this reason the present commentary is also an exercise in the history of theology. On the other hand it also presumes, rashly no doubt, to be part of the ongoing and larger theological enterprise of Holy Church in our own times. For this reason I am daunted by the challenge published by Father M.-D. Chenu about a half-century ago: "In a way, the history of theology falls within theology itself. A perfect history of theology, if one existed, would yield a theology of history" (from the Introduction to his *La théologie au douzième siècle*).

History and Worship

We reflected earlier on Ben Sirach's list of "famous men," which forms a continuous narrative by a series of very short biographies. Similar to that list is the roll call of the heroes of faith in Hebrews 11. Like the list in Ben Sirach, this one too includes Enoch, Noah, and Abraham near the beginning. More pertinent to our reflections here, however, is the place where the narrative ends—in a scene of liturgical worship. The author ends his narrative by referring to this "so great a cloud of witnesses" (12:1), who appear shortly afterwards in his description of orthodox Christian worship:

> But you have come to Mount Zion and to the city of the living God, the heavenly Jerusalem, to an innumerable company of angels, to the general assembly and church of the firstborn *who are* registered in heaven, to God the Judge of all, to the spirits of just men made perfect, to Jesus the Mediator of the new covenant, and to the blood of sprinkling that speaks better things than *that of* Abel (Heb. 12:22–24).

In this memorable text, the history of the chosen people comes to its fulfillment when in one assembly is gathered together the entire "cloud of witnesses," those "spirits of just men made perfect," along with Christians themselves, these later pilgrims who have "come to Mount Zion and to the city of the living God." Once again, biblical history arrives at its culmination in God's people assembled to worship Him. In our worship we are surrounded by, and enter into communion with, the great cloud of the biblical witnesses, those "spirits of just men made perfect." In our worship, biblical history is *now*. It has never stopped, and our own lives are part of it.

When the saints on earth worship the Lord, that is to say, this worship joins them to the worship in heaven. The prayers offered by the Church on earth are mingled with the worship in heaven: "Then another angel, having a golden censer, came and stood at the altar. He was given much incense, that he should offer *it* with the prayers of all the saints upon the golden altar which was before the throne. And the smoke of the incense, with the prayers of the saints, ascended before God from the angel's hand" (Rev. 8:3–4).

But what happens then on the earth? These prayers jointly offered by the saints in heaven and on earth affect the course of history. Things *happen* in history: "Then the angel took the censer, filled it with fire from the altar, and threw *it* to the earth. And there were noises, thunderings, lightnings, and an earthquake" (8:5), and the following chapters of Revelation go on to describe the historical results of this prayer.

The Church's worship, then, is at the center of the Church's place in history. It is through her orthodox glorification of the biblical God, the Father of her Lord Jesus Christ, that the Church chiefly fulfills the historical role to which that God has summoned her.

Finally, it is in this worship of the Church that Holy Scripture itself finds its complete and proper context. It is chiefly through its proclamation in the worship of the Church, centered on the sacraments of the Church and most especially the eucharistic liturgy, that the Bible gives shape, substance, meaning, and hope to man's history.

1 CHRONICLES 1

જી

IN FIRST CHRONICLES THE PREMONARCHICAL PART of human history (that
is, the long period from the beginning of the world to the reign of
David, which latter began about 1000 BC) is reduced to hardly more
than an outline, in some places simply a list of names (chapters 1–9).
There will be many such lists throughout Chronicles.

By leaving out the details of human history prior to David's monarchy, the Chronicler conveys the impression that everything that happened prior to David was a preparation for the covenant God made
with Israel's first true king.

Indeed, for the Chronicler the *real* covenant of the Lord is that
which He made with David. All the earlier covenants (with Noah, with
Abraham, and even with Moses) appear diminished by comparison. This
is a perspective unique to the Chronicler. David is his interpretive lens.

This explains the Chronicler's lack of interest in the kingdom of
Israel, that northern entity established by Jeroboam I at the death of
Solomon in 922. Indeed, if the Chronicler does not regard the found-
ing of the short-lived Northern Kingdom, the schismatic kingdom of
Israel (922–722), with so much as an explicit mention, it is precisely
because that kingdom was founded in opposition to the Davidic covenant. As we shall see when we come to that period, the Chronicler's
theological preoccupations render his stories very different from those
in the Books of Kings, where some of the more memorable stories are,
in fact, about the monarchs and prophets of the north.

The genealogies of this first chapter are concentrated on the descendants of Abraham, who dominate the Arabian Peninsula and the western part of the Fertile Crescent (vv. 27–54). We detect that the author is
narrowing his focus, concentrating his energies toward the goal of the
narrative, which is David.

For all that concentration, nonetheless, the Chronicler does place
the history of Israel within more ample human history. Thus, he
commences with Adam, the single father of the human race, and his

extensive genealogies of early man give what one historian calls "evidence of an ecumenical concern." Israel's history is regarded as the high point of human history. Later on, the New Testament will, in a similar way, extend this perspective by tracing the genealogy of Jesus all the way back to Adam (Luke 3:23–38).

Somewhat in contrast to this "ecumenical interest," however, the genealogical lists in this first chapter also reflect the Chronicler's concern for the purity of Israel's own bloodline. Religious leaders in postexilic Judaism (that is, after 539 BC)—and no one more than Ezra himself—were very much preoccupied with this bloodline purity, out of a need to maintain the nation's ethnic and religious integrity. This is why we find in the Books of Ezra and Nehemiah, works following the theological traits of Chronicles, a solidly negative attitude toward the Samaritans or any marriage with non-Israelites.

The lists here in chapter 1, then, serving the theological interests of the Chronicler, were not intended to be complete, and we should avoid attempts to reconcile these lists with other genealogical material, as though their incompleteness were somehow an historical defect. As St. Augustine noted repeatedly in *The City of God*, none of the genealogies in the Bible was meant to be exhaustive. Each biblical genealogy, Augustine saw, served a specific literary, historical, and theological purpose. A good reading of the Holy Scriptures should concentrate on discovering those purposes.

In the present narrative, for example, Cain and all his descendants are omitted. Why? In fact, the Chronicler refuses even to mention the existence of Cain's posterity for the same reason that he will later ignore the schismatic kings of the North—namely, why should he bother to recall what the Lord has chosen to forget? Hence, the Chronicler writes here only of those ancients who were important to the ancestry and family history of the chosen people. This interest determines his choice of material.

Respecting the present list we observe that, of the three sons of Noah, there are fourteen names associated with Japheth (vv. 5–7), thirty with Ham (vv. 8–16), and twenty-six with Shem (vv. 17–24). Thus, the list consists of seventy peoples or nations. The Bible is fond of selections of seventy (Num. 11:16; Luke 10:1), which is the sum reached by the multiplication of the digital ten by the perfect number, seven (which is "perfect" because it comes from the union of the divine three with the human four—man himself having four sides and thus dividing the world into four directions).

How should the Christian read this list of names? First, he should see them as pertaining to his own family history. Second, he should regard them as the names in that "great cloud of witnesses." If they tend to become blurry, he does well to remember that a certain blurriness is characteristic of clouds. The reader should not think of this as a problem. Third, let the Christian reader devoutly pray that his own name will be added to this ancient list. If he bears these considerations in mind, it is unlikely that the task of reading these countless names will ever become boring.

1 CHRONICLES 2

ॐ

Now we begin the genealogies of the "Israelites." Indeed, we here observe, for the first time, that Chronicles habitually refers to Jacob by the name "Israel," the name he received after his famous wrestling match at Peniel (v. 1). Whereas the name Jacob denotes that intriguing historical character to whom so many interesting things happened, the name Israel denotes more particularly the patriarch of the twelve tribes, the man who gave them his name. The Chronicler omits all the fascinating stories about "Jacob," but he is extremely interested in this same character under the name "Israel."

In the genealogies of Chronicles, beginning with this chapter, we also observe that great prominence and elaboration are accorded the tribes of Judah and Levi, the kingly and priestly households. Taking the genealogies of Chronicles as a whole, Judah will get 102 verses and Levi 81 verses of attention, whereas all the other tribes taken together will receive only 126 verses.

In this respect these genealogies contribute to a more general theme in the Books of Chronicles. For the Chronicler, writing long after the destruction of the Northern Kingdom by the Assyrians in 722 BC, only the tribes of Judah and Levi were of immediate moment, and he was eager to demonstrate the mutual support of the priestly family and the covenanted royal house of David. Hence, this dominance of Levi and Judah in his genealogies.

The present chapter also provides the Bible's only list of the Jerahmeelites (vv. 25–41), David's "country cousins" mentioned in 1 Samuel 27:10; 30:29. As usual, the Chronicler is interested in this family solely because of its relationship to David.

This pronounced accent on the genealogy of Judah will be of even more significance to the Christian, of course, because this is the genealogy of the Incarnation itself: "For *it is* evident that our Lord arose from Judah" (Heb. 7:14).

Within the genealogy of Judah, special prominence is given to the ancestors of David's father Jesse (vv. 10–12), for obvious reasons, and then to his descendants (vv. 13–15). Here we learn that Jesse had seven sons, which is a problem if we recall that 1 Samuel 16:6–11 mentions eight sons of Jesse. Perhaps the rabbis were correct in their speculation that one of the eight sons, having died childless, is intentionally left out of this genealogy.

Because of Caleb's prominence within the territory of Judah, a great deal of this chapter concerns his family (vv. 18–24, 42–50). There is, however, another reason for this attention given to the family of Caleb. It provides some background for the character of Bezalel mentioned in 2 Chronicles 1:5. This Bezalel was of interest to the Chronicler because he was the craftsman credited with the proper embellishment of the tabernacle (Ex. 31:35–38). In this genealogy of Caleb, then, we see another sign of the Chronicler's concern for all things associated with worship.

Since the word *kenite* means "smith," we have in verses 50–55 the world's first genealogy of, well, "the Smith family." Let the attentive reader, then, see what he can do to "keep up with the Smiths." They too are in the Book of Life.

1 CHRONICLES 3

WE NOW BEGIN THE LIST OF THE ROYAL LINE OF DAVID, which this chapter extends to at least the beginning of the fourth century before Christ. This latter fact does not necessarily prove anything about the date of the composition of Chronicles, because it is quite conceivable that a later editor or copyist of Chronicles may have extended the list.

In this respect one does well to bear in mind that Chronicles was "canonized" into the Old Testament rather late in Jewish history, so that no earlier editor or copyist would have scrupled to augment the text. In fact, the ancient Greek translation (Septuagint) of this chapter extends the list all the way to about 250 BC, exactly the period in which the Septuagint translation was being made.

The sacred text names the mothers of the six sons David fathered in Hebron, before the removal of his capital to Jerusalem in 993 (vv. 1–4). This detail is curious, because Chronicles otherwise omits the fact that David's reign was not recognized by the northern tribes for the first seven years (cf. 2 Sam. 5:5). This omission, in turn, is consistent with the Chronicler's general disregard for the politics of the northern tribes.

Did the birth of these first six sons at Hebron diminish their claims to succeed David on the throne? Perhaps, but we must bear in mind that the rules for royal succession in Israel—kingship being a completely new thing for the nation—were not yet established, so there is no reason to suppose that the royal succession was expected to follow the principle of primogeniture.

The Bathshua of verse 5 is, of course, Bathsheba. (In accord with Chronicles' sustained effort to edify, on which we have already commented, David's adultery with her is not mentioned.) The reference to three sons of Bathsheba older than Solomon is unexpected. In the light of 2 Samuel 12:24 ("Then David comforted Bathsheba his wife, and went in to her and lay with her. So she bore a son, and he called his name Solomon"), we would not have anticipated such a detail.

The passage of the royal line to Solomon and his descendants is recorded in verse 10. Through verse 16, these Davidic kings are listed up until the fall of Jerusalem to the Babylonians in 587 BC.

The exilic and postexilic descendants of the royal household, listed here so thoroughly (vv. 17–24), bear witness to the careful maintenance of records among the Jews of the sixth and fifth centuries. The Book of Ezra will further testify to this care.

The later names in this list, especially after Zerubbabel (v. 19), are difficult to reconcile with the genealogies in Matthew 1 and Luke 3. The writer of the present commentary is happy to leave this difficulty to the investigation of those with the interest and patience to resolve it.

This chapter, then, is the beginning of the royal line of David, the progeny of promise. Here the author's attention is directed more especially to the genealogy we recognize as fulfilled in Jesus the Lord. This is the chapter that prepares more immediately for Christmas.

1 CHRONICLES 4

ॐ

WE HAVE ALREADY REMARKED THAT THE GENEALOGIES in Chronicles are considerably more detailed for the tribes of Judah and Levi than for any of the others. The present chapter (vv. 1–23) on the tribe of Judah illustrates the point.

To grasp the historical reason for this emphasis, it is sufficient to reflect that the Southern Kingdom, the realm of Judah, had an unbroken succession of a single dynasty (the six years of Athaliah's usurpation being only a blip on the screen) from about 1000 to 587 BC. During more than four centuries, beginning in 993, this kingdom had its capital in a single city, Jerusalem. This stability and continuity of Judah contributed in no small measure to the better preservation of its historical memory through archived records.

In these respects Judah is to be contrasted with the Northern Kingdom, Israel, which was governed by a series of dynasties, some of them very short, over a period of only two centuries (922–722). That kingdom's capital, moreover, did not remain in a single place during that time. The kingdom of Israel's instability and impermanence are further reflected in the relative paucity of its preserved records. Sometimes, indeed, even the identity of individual northern kings was lost from the stories about their reigns. For example, 2 Kings 5 does not tell us the name of the northern king to whom the Syrian king sent Naaman in order to be cleansed of his leprosy. Modern scholars may speculate on the question, but if the author of Kings had known that person's identity, he would surely have given it.

In short, the final and dominating perspective of the Old Testament is that of Judah, not the Northern Kingdom. Judah's own records, therefore, are far better preserved, Judah's history being more immediate and proximate to the Bible's composition. Judah, then, and not northern Israel, represents the true continuity of biblical history, and nowhere is this fact more evident than in Chronicles.

Some of the sources cited in this chapter appear to be very old, as the text itself claims (v. 22). Indeed, the expression "to this day" (vv. 41,

43) seems to refer, not to the time of the Chronicler, but to the period of these older sources that he is citing word-for-word. This is clear from the reference to the Amalekites, who were long gone by the time the Chronicler wrote of them.

With respect to Jabez we observe that his name involves a play on words. His mother, we read, bore him in "pain"—*jozeb*—so his name was derived from a switching around of letters. We also note that the prayer of Jabez which the Lord heard was concerned with the avoidance of future pain (v. 10). There is no reason to suppose that there is anything especially efficacious, much less miraculous, about the prayer of Jabez.

The region of Judah contained the least fertile soil in all the Holy Land. Therefore, it does not surprise us that the tribe of Judah, where men may sometimes have felt absolutely desperate as farmers, produced so many craftsmen (v. 14), linen workers (v. 21), and potters. This last group was in the royal employ (v. 23).

The tribes of Reuben and Simeon, because they were situated in the south, were in some measure absorbed into the political life of Judah. This is why their records are listed next (4:24—5:10).

In case the reader has not figured it out, let us note that the Chelub of verse 11 is Caleb.

The events of verse 41 will be explained in 2 Chronicles 20.

In the present chapter we gain some sense of the danger of *schism*, a Greek word that means a rip or tear. Schism is a rift in the social continuity of redemptive history; it can place entire populations outside of the covenant made with David and consummated in Christ. Since the Church, as "the pillar and ground of the truth" (1 Tim. 3:15), is the only institution on earth with the authority to interpret the teaching of the Bible, separation from the Church is effectively separation from the Holy Scriptures. Schism, even when it claims biblical authority, actually represents a rupture from biblical history.

1 CHRONICLES 5

THIS CHAPTER BEGINS WITH A BRIEF EXPLANATION of why Reuben, though Israel's eldest son, did not inherit nor transmit the right of primogeniture. (In fact, however, throughout the Bible, God's favorable choice most often seems to fall elsewhere than on the eldest son.) The reasons given here reflect the narratives in Genesis 35:22; 49:4.

Even while admitting the transferral of Israel's birthright to Joseph, the Chronicler feels compelled to mention that Judah was the strong tribe that produced the leader (*nagid*) of God's people (v. 2; the same word is used in 2 Sam. 7:8).

Dealing with Reuben's settlements east of the Jordan and Dead Sea (v. 8) apparently prompts the author's mind to remain in that general location and discuss the tribe of Gad (vv. 11–17) and the half-tribe of Manasseh (vv. 23–24), which also settled in Gilead and Bashan. This sequence interrupts the author's pattern of adhering to lists of the sons as they appear in Genesis 46:16 or Numbers 26:15–18.

The mention of Sharon in verse 16 is most mysterious, because the Plain of Sharon is nowhere near that area.

In verse 17 the author traces his source material to a census made in the mid-eighth century.

This chapter has two notices of wars against the Hagrites, Arabian groups living east of the Jordan, one in the late eleventh century (v. 10) and one at an apparently later period (vv. 19–20). The Hagrites, twice defeated, were hardly destroyed. We find them later in the Greek writers Strabo and Ptolemy and the Latin author Pliny.

Some elements in this account suggest a source as early as the ninth century. For example, we know the towns of Aroer, Baalmeon, and Nebo (v. 8) fell under Moabite control during that century.

The chapter's closing verses (25–26) indicate the irony that these eastern tribes, victorious in war by God's favor, nonetheless succumbed to the religion of those whom they defeated. This explains their massive deportation by Tiglath-pileser in 734. (The material here is drawn from 2 Kings 15:19, 29; 17:6; 18:11.) Thus, an Assyrian emperor is portrayed as an instrument in the hand of the supreme Lord of history.

This chapter hints at God's use of world history to chasten His own people. In biblical times He accomplished this through the Egyptians, the Assyrians, the Babylonians, the Persians, the Greeks, and the Romans. In later times the Lord has done this through such instruments as the Huns, the Goths, the Saracens, the Seljuks, the Ottomans, and the Bolsheviks.

1 CHRONICLES 6

&

NEXT INTO CONSIDERATION COME THE SONS OF LEVI, the priestly tribe. The list is not complete, and we observe a certain stylization as the genealogy begins. Leaving out such names as Jehoiada (who will be prominent in 2 Chr. 23—24) and Uriah (who will appear in Ezra 8:33), this list contains twelve priestly generations from Aaron to the Solomonic temple (vv. 1–10) and another twelve generations from that temple to the postexilic temple (vv. 11–15; Ezra 3:2). In due course we shall see that twenty-four was the number of the priestly families, an image reflected in Revelation 4:10. (There is a continuation of the postexilic list in Neh. 12:10.)

As the previous chapter spoke of the Assyrian Tiglath-pileser as God's historical instrument against the Northern Kingdom (5:26), so the present chapter once again sees the hand of God at work in Judah's own exile to Babylon (v. 15). This perspective reveals the author's theology of history.

In the section on the Levites (vv. 16–30) the most notable feature is the author's inclusion of Elkanah and his son Samuel in the Levitical line (vv. 23–26). This section throws light on the beginning of 1 Samuel, which describes Elkanah's family as Ephraimite. From the present text it is clear that Elkanah's was a Levitical family living in the territory of Ephraim. Since the Levites were deliberately spread around among the various tribes, this is not surprising.

The listing of the Levitical singers (vv. 31–48) is unusually detailed, suggesting that the author had access to more ample source material for this section. It is not unreasonable, in fact, to think that the Chronicler may have had recourse to memories, and perhaps even written archives, handed down in his own family.

David, whom we otherwise know to have taken a particular interest in music (1 Sam. 16:18–23; 2 Sam. 1:17–27), is credited with the inspiration and organization of Israel's program of liturgical music (v. 31). The Chronicler comes back to this thesis repeatedly (15:16, 27; 25:1;

2 Chr. 29:26; Neh. 12:46), and we might suspect as much from the Book of Psalms.

Although Korah was punished for rebellion against Aaron (Num. 16:16), his descendants (v. 37) served as Levitical musicians and are credited with compiling some of the Book of Psalms (42—49, 84—88). The Asaph in verse 39 is also well known in the Psalms (73—83).

The Zadokites, the descendants of Zadok (v. 53), became the chief priestly family at the time of David, who is the true hero of the Books of Chronicles. Although it is clear in 2 Samuel that Zadok was the chief priest at the time of David, only Chronicles (vv. 49–53) provides us with his earlier lineage.

In the New Testament the Zadokites are called "Sadducees." They were leaders among those who rejected David's final Heir, a tragedy that clearly would have distressed the Chronicler.

The Levites were not given a special tribal portion of the Holy Land like the other tribes, but were dispersed throughout the tribes, so that the latter would benefit from their priestly ministry (vv. 54–81). The Levites were allotted specific cities among the tribes, the first being the ancient shrine of Hebron (v. 55), which was also appointed as a city of refuge (v. 57). Indeed, we observe that all the major cities of the Holy Land, except Jerusalem, were designated as priestly cities—Debir, Bethshemesh, Anathoth, Shechem, Gezer, Aijalon, Golan, Ramoth (both of them), Kadesh, Tabor, and so forth.

The sons of Aaron received property near Jerusalem, so as always to be available for service in the capital (vv. 54–55). To accommodate this arrangement, special provisions were made with the family of Caleb, which also inherited property in that region (v. 56).

The "clergy" in this chapter are not constituted as a separate class living apart from the rest of Israel. They are to live among the various Israelite tribes precisely in order to be of service to them. In the ministries of the New Testament this process is taken a step further. The bishops, presbyters, and deacons of the Church are not drawn from a single tribe or family, and the transmission of their ministries is not according to bloodlines.

1 CHRONICLES 7

ALTHOUGH OUR AUTHOR HAS NO INTEREST in the Northern Kingdom as a political entity, he does preserve for us a considerable record of the early history of the northern *tribes*, in which his interest is consistently sharp. Indeed, even though the material available to him must have been sparse, the Chronicler seems to have used it all, because there are details in the present chapter not to be found elsewhere in Holy Scripture.

The Chronicler used what records he had. For some of these tribes (Naphtali, for instance) the author had hardly more at his disposal than the lists in Genesis 46 and Numbers 26. Many census records of the Northern Kingdom had perished at Israel's fall to the Assyrians in 722.

The specific details of the tribe of Issachar (vv. 1–7) come from Genesis 46:13 and Numbers 26:23–25. The numbers given here, however, are quite a bit higher than those indicated in the census of Numbers 1 and 26.

Something should be said about the numbers themselves, because at first reading they seem far too high for the fairly small area of the Holy Land. To gain a more realistic assessment of the situation, it is useful to bear in mind that the Hebrew word for "thousand," *'eleph*, is actually a subdivision of a tribe, the numerical count of which varied a great deal but seldom came to a full thousand. In the biblical context *'eleph* indicates a military unit, comparable to our "battalion," "regiment," or "brigade." If this military context of the expression is borne in mind, the very high numbers in this chapter are rendered much more plausible.

Although the Hebrew text of verses 7–11 indicates the tribe of Benjamin, this reading most certainly comes from a copyist's error (*bene zebulun*, or "sons of Zebulon," was mistaken for *ben-jamin*) and later was appropriately corrected in one of the Greek manuscripts to read "Zebulon" instead of Benjamin. This is the usual sequence, after all, in which Holy Scripture refers to Zebulon, nor would there be any mention of Zebulon in the entire list in 1 Chronicles unless it were here. Moreover, the names given here do not correspond to the Benjamite names in chapter 8, nor in Genesis 46:21, nor in Numbers 26:38.

As we know from Genesis 49:13, Zebulon was situated on the sea-shore, just under Phoenicia, and perhaps this fact is reflected in the name "Tarshish" in verse 10, the same name as that ancient port (Cadiz) beyond the Straits of Gibraltar, from which ships came to the Middle East from the other end of the Mediterranean. In short, we read this section as referring to Zebulon, not Benjamin.

Similarly, verse 12 appears to refer to the tribe of Dan, inasmuch as Hushim is identified in Genesis 46:23 as a son of Dan. Dan's name seems to have dropped out of the text by a scribal error. (In Hebrew the name has only two letters, somewhat similar in shape.)

The Naphtali list in verse 13 is identical with Genesis 46:24. It appears that the Chronicler had access to no records about Naphtali except this Genesis text and Numbers 26:48.

The Manasseh list (vv. 14–19) includes both parts of that tribe and indicates its relationship to Syria. In this section on Manasseh it is clear that the Hebrew women became wives for the Syrian over-lords, indicating that the half-tribe of Manasseh that lived east of the Jordan had become simply a political extension of Syria. As such, it suffered the fate of Syria when Tiglath-pileser's army showed up in 734.

In the large tribe of Ephraim (vv. 20–29), the most notable person is Joshua (v. 27). The mention of the slaying of the sons of Ephraim by Philistine raiders (vv. 20–21) suggests that the Chronicler had access to a very early source. This section is also the only place in the Bible where a woman is said to have founded a city (v. 24).

Although the tribe of Asher (vv. 30–40) is unusually ample with personal names, a third of them being found only here, there are no place names. Asher sat geographically furthest from Jerusalem.

After this rather sketchy outline of the northern tribes, the author is now ready to speak of the tribe of Benjamin, situated on the border between the north and the south in the Holy Land. Since Benjamin is the tribe of Saul, Israel's first king, the author will use this treatment to move from pure listing to a narrative of the kingdom, which David will assume in due course. The next chapter will begin, therefore, with the list of the Benjamites.

When we dig a hole with a shovel, the hole at the top is regularly wider than at the bottom. The Chronicler has begun with a fairly wide opening in the hole. Now that he has dealt with all the tribes, he is ready to narrow his focus, so as to begin soon his narrative proper. When he arrives at Benjamin, he will be nearly there.

1 CHRONICLES 8

JUST AS THE OPENING GENEALOGIES OF 1 CHRONICLES emphasized David, so these genealogies at the end concentrate on Saul. Thus, this final listing is of Saul's own tribe, Benjamin.

The initial list given in the present text (vv. 1–28) is drawn partly from Genesis 46:21 and Numbers 26:38–40, but there are discrepancies. Indeed, no other part of Chronicles is so full of textual difficulties as this section. Someone has suggested—and the suggestion is plausible—that the ancient scribes, having copied out seven whole chapters containing almost nothing but names, were suffering from unusual fatigue and ennui! Hence, we have an unusual number of transcriptional errors. Perhaps so, but there is really nothing to be done about it. The various hypothetical emendations suggested by textual scholars seem rather shaky. We must resign ourselves to a bit of unavoidable obscurity in this chapter.

We recognize Ehud (v. 6) as the left-handed judge from this right-handed (*ben-jamini*) tribe (Judg. 3:12–30).

Jerusalem, now introduced in verses 28 and 32, will be treated at length in the following chapter.

Although the author's intent in verses 29–40 was to present Saul's ancestry and lineage, the method is not direct or straightforward. After presenting Jeiel (cf. 9:5) and his progeny, he moves to Saul's immediate family, which does not seem to be connected to Jeiel. Even the relationships portrayed here among Abner, Kish, Ner, and Saul are difficult to reconcile with 1 Samuel 14:50–51. We must bear in mind—for certainly the author of 1 Chronicles bore in mind—that this was the family that was ultimately rejected and replaced by David's.

For all that, the Chronicler himself seems to have been faithful to very old sources here, sources independent of 2 Samuel. We may illustrate this by his retention of the name of the pagan god "Baal" in two of the names given here, Ethbaal and Meribbaal (vv. 33–34). This is curious and historically significant. In 2 Samuel (2:8; 9:2) these names were changed to Ishbosheth and Mephibosheth.

Why the change in 2 Samuel and not in 2 Chronicles? The answer, though easy, tells us something of canonical history. Second Samuel is contained in the second section of the Hebrew Bible, the *Nebiwim*, or "Prophets." These books were regularly read in the synagogue. Reluctant to use the name of a pagan god, Baal, in the synagogue, the reader customarily changed the name to *bosheth*, meaning "shame." This practice led to the same change being made in the text itself. There was no need to make such a change in the Books of Chronicles, however, which are found in the third section of the Hebrew Old Testament, the *Ketubim*, or "Writings." This section was not placed in the biblical canon until later, and Chronicles was not read publicly in the synagogue. Hence, Chronicles has preserved the old form of these two names.

We should notice, in this process, that the transmission of the Bible is inseparable from its use in worship. This fact is important as a principle of interpretation in all parts of Holy Scripture.

1 CHRONICLES 9

WE HAVE NOW COMPLETED THE GENEALOGIES of "all Israel," the name the Chronicler prefers to designate the whole chosen people as distinct from the Northern Kingdom, known as "Israel" in the Books of Kings. For the Chronicler the phrase "all Israel" is full of deep religious feeling, as when it serves to describe the religious reforms of King Hezekiah three centuries later (2 Chr. 30:1, 5).

As we have seen, the author of Chronicles was careful to treat last the tribe of Benjamin and the house of Saul among the sons of Israel, because this sequence permitted him to move almost seamlessly from mere lists to real narrative. Likewise, this order makes it an easy step for him now to go to Jerusalem, which sat on the southern border of the tribe of Benjamin.

Jerusalem had not been part of the land inherited by the twelve tribes at the time of Joshua. It remained a Canaanite (or, more specifically, a Jebusite) stronghold until taken by David's forces in 992 BC and made the capital of the united kingdom (2 Sam. 5:6–7). This is why we find Jerusalem, unlike the other cities of the Promised Land, inhabited by Israelites from several of the tribes (v. 3).

Because the ark of the covenant was transferred to Jerusalem shortly after it became David's capital, the city was quickly transformed into a religious center, a whole generation before Solomon's construction of the temple there. Hence, it is scarcely surprising that the capital was home to a high number of priests, Levites, and other liturgical ministers (vv. 10–22).

The Chronicler describes their several responsibilities (vv. 23–34). In this inventory he gives special prominence to the temple's musicians (vv. 14–16), who are listed immediately after the priests (vv. 10–13). The Chronicler leaves no doubt about his great respect for the ministry of the temple choir. Its leaders (6:39; 16:14) were Asaph (v. 15) and Jeduthun (v. 16).

The gatekeepers, especially delegated to preserve holiness within the temple, were to emulate that great champion of Israel's holiness, the priest Phineas (v. 20).

The sections of the text concerning the singers and gatekeepers, we note, are arranged in chiastic order:

A—order of singers (vv. 14–16)

B—order of gatekeepers (vv. 17–27)

B'—duties of gatekeepers (vv. 28–32)

A'—duties of singers (vv. 33–34)

In verse 35 the author returns to the genealogy of Saul, in order to prepare for the battle of Gilboa (1000 BC) at the beginning of the next chapter. It is at the death of Saul in that battle that David assumes the throne.

All is now prepared for the narrative proper. The priests and Levites are in place; the ark of the covenant has been introduced; the choir is ready. It is time to start.

1 CHRONICLES 10

THIS SUCCINCT ACCOUNT OF THE BATTLE OF GILBOA may be supplemented by the accounts in 1 Samuel 31 and Josephus, *The Antiquities of the Jews* 6.14.7–9.

The chapter opens abruptly. After all the genealogies, lists, rosters, and schedules of the previous nine chapters, the reader is suddenly confronted with a story of combat, in which the whole battle is over in one verse: "Now the Philistines fought against Israel; and the men of Israel fled from before the Philistines, and fell slain on Mount Gilboa" (v. 1).

There is no need, however, to ascribe the first nine chapters to a different hand, as some have suggested. Indeed, there are two sound reasons to resist this hypothetical ascription. First, the ideas, themes, and preoccupations of those first nine chapters are identical to those in the rest of Chronicles. Second, if the opening of the present chapter seems abrupt, it would hardly appear less abrupt as the beginning of a book. Even the hack novelist will do his readers the kindness of remarking that "it was a dark and stormy night" before announcing that "suddenly a shot rang out."

Following a pattern we have now come to expect, the Chronicler has nothing good to say for Saul. The latter's sole significance was that his downfall prepared the way for David. Consequently, the book's actual narrative commences with Saul's downfall at the battle of Gilboa, bringing Saul's twenty years of reign to an end. Although the wounded Saul died by his own hand, it was really the Lord who slew him (v. 14).

Saul is condemned for his "unfaithfulness" (v. 13). The Chronicler uses this same word (*ma'al*) to explain why the nation was deported to Babylon (9:1; 2 Chr. 36:14), and he will employ it to describe the later reigns of Ahaz (2 Chr. 28:19; 29:19) and Manasseh (2 Chr. 33:19). Thus, Saul's unfaithfulness is for the Chronicler part of the larger theme of the nation's unfaithfulness.

The assertion that all of Saul's family perished (v. 7) must be understood in a sense compatible with the subsequent seven years' reign of Ishbosheth in the north (2 Sam. 2—3) and the survival of Mephibosheth

(2 Sam. 9:7; 16:3). Perhaps the Chronicler intends to include here the deaths of those men years later. In fact, he has already listed other sons of Saul in 9:39–40.

Even though the Chronicler has nothing good to say for Saul, he does record the fact that some of Saul's contemporaries took a different view (v. 12).

The Chronicler's negative account of Saul is important to his history as a whole, because it serves as a contrast to the Lord's choice of David. In the Bible there is no such thing as history without "election." It is the Lord's "election" that gives structure and substance to history. Otherwise the deeds of men are simply an amorphous blob, of which they can make no reliable sense. Without the true Lord of history, a Lord who makes choices and assigns vocations, human history is as formless as a jungle.

1 CHRONICLES 11

୬ଡ଼

THE MATERIAL IN THIS CHAPTER IS DRAWN from two widely separated parts of 2 Samuel. Verses 1–9 reflect the material in 2 Samuel 5:1–10, while verses 10–47 come from 2 Samuel 23:8–39.

The Chronicler greatly abbreviates the lengthy, difficult, and complicated story of David's gaining control over all the tribes. We note that the material in the first four chapters of 2 Samuel is simply missing. There is no mention of the brief reign of Ishbosheth, the crisis of Abner, the subsequent negotiations, and Joab's hand in Abner's death. Instead, the story skips immediately to the gathering of the tribes at Hebron (David's first capital, before the capture of Jerusalem) to make David the king. There is no suggestion that Israel was politically divided between north and south (a division that would reappear at Solomon's death in 922). Indeed, in place of "all the tribes of Israel" in 2 Samuel 5:1, we now have simply "all Israel" in verse 1. That is to say, the nation is completely united; even the tribal distinctions are lost. Thus, Jerusalem is captured by "David and all Israel" (v. 4).

Having thus described David's rise to power and the taking of Jerusalem in a bare nine verses of narrative, the Chronicler returns to what we have begun to suspect he does best—he provides more lists of names! This time, however, the lists are in large part derived from 2 Samuel 23:8–39.

First, there are David's "three mighty men" (vv. 10–14). Since only two names are given, however, we might suspect that Joab, treated in the previous verses, was to be understood as included among them. It is more plausible, however, to suspect a copyist's omission, since the name given in 2 Samuel 23:11 is Shammah.

Second, there is a list of thirty other warriors of renown (vv. 20–47). Whereas the corresponding list in 2 Samuel ends with Uriah the Hittite, the Chronicler adds several names more (vv. 41–47). Since these men appear to come predominantly from the east side of the Jordan, we may presume that the Chronicler received their names from a Transjordanian source not available to the author of Samuel.

Such lists of combatants reflect the period when warfare was generally conducted hand to hand. In our own times, when weapons are employed from great distances, it is difficult to imagine this impression of ongoing hand-to-hand combat. Indeed, Shelby Foote, the preeminent historian of the Civil War, remarked that that war produced relatively few casualties from the bayonet; most wounds were inflicted by gunfire at a distance. In very ancient accounts of combat, however, such as that between David and Goliath in 1 Samuel 17 and many places in Homer, the reader sometimes has the impression that any given battle was just a series of private fights between individuals. These biblical lists of warriors reflect that same setting. In fact, even Josephus, writing during the period of the New Testament, saw no reason to include these lists.

With David, says the Chronicler, was "the Lord of hosts," a title that fits the military character of the whole chapter.

Especially curious is the place of Joab in this narrative. First, this text is the only place in Holy Scripture that explains how he came to be David's chief commander (vv. 6–7). Second, only this text speaks of Joab's role in the repair and reconstruction of Jerusalem (v. 8). Third, Joab is never criticized in Chronicles, which even omits David's final curse on him (1 Kings 2:5).

1 CHRONICLES 12

THE MILITARY LISTS GO ON! As we reflected in the previous chapter, in the days when hand-to-hand combat was the normal way of warfare, it was natural that a certain individual notoriety attached to warriors of great skill with sword, javelin, and battle-ax. This is why we find lists of famous warriors in the ancient literature of warfare.

We may take the *Iliad* as a well-known instance. In his descriptions of the various battles at the gates of Troy, Homer emphasized the valor and prowess of individual warriors such as Achilles, Hector, Ajax, and so on. One-on-one combat was the rule, and the stories of the combat delineate the efforts of individual brave men.

Holy Scripture comes from that same era and demonstrates that same preoccupation. The story of David and Goliath in 1 Samuel 17, for example, complete with the speeches of each man prior to their engagement, will support comparison with the accounts of Patroclus and Hector, Diomede and Aeneas, and so on.

What we have at the end of 1 Chronicles 11 and through chapter 12 are similar lists of outstanding famous warriors who threw in their lot with David. They are drawn, as we can see, from among the cream of their own tribes, Benjamin (vv. 1–7), Gad (vv. 8–15), Manasseh (vv. 19–22), and so on. This attention to the individual tribes represented in David's band helps to emphasize that David was the choice of "all Israel."

Because they came to David from Saul's own tribe, the warriors of Benjamin are mentioned first (vv. 1–7). In fact, when the other tribes eventually rebelled against the house of David in 922 (an event that the Chronicler will not honor with so much as a mention), the tribe of Benjamin remained loyal. In the present text, attention is given to the very specialized and ambidextrous skills of the Benjamites.

The warriors of Gad (vv. 8–15), who may have joined David during his sojourn at Engedi (1 Sam. 24:1), had the "faces of lions," an expression that probably means they looked fierce to their opponents. It was not all show, however, because these warriors, in addition to their speed, were accomplished swimmers, able to cross the cold, swollen waters of the Jordan at flood stage.

All these men came to strengthen the army of David and secure his throne over all Israel (v. 38). This union of all the tribes remained for the Chronicler an ideal that King Hezekiah would later attempt to restore (2 Chr. 30—31).

In the midst of this impressive list, and in order to make him the representative of the whole lot, "the Spirit came upon Amisai, chief of the captains" (v. 18). "*We are* yours, O David" expresses the enthusiasm of the whole kingdom. Amisai speaks not only for Israel, but more especially for the Chronicler, for whom the Lord's covenant with David was *the* covenant of history.

The Christian reader, pursuing the sacred text with the Christian Church, will see in this preoccupation a deeper Christological significance. If the covenant with David is *the* covenant, the reason for this is great David's greater Son, in whom God is bound to the human race in that irrevocable manner called the hypostatic union. This is the more profound meaning of the oath God swore to David, promising that the line of David would *never* be deprived of David's throne. David's Son and Lord sits forever enthroned in glory, and the Chronicler's list of warriors is simply the initial count of those who throughout history will rally with prophetic enthusiasm to David's throne.

1 CHRONICLES 13

❧

IN 2 SAMUEL 5:11–25 DAVID FIRST BUILDS HIS OWN HOUSE and does combat against the Philistines, before beginning to make Jerusalem the religious center of the kingdom. The Chronicler, however, more interested in theological principle than in historical sequence, postpones that narrative in order to concentrate on Jerusalem's theological importance. He first tells the story of David's attempt to bring the ark of the covenant to Jerusalem.

Since the destruction of the ancient shrine at Shiloh, when Samuel was but a child, the ark had apparently been a bit neglected (v. 3). As a religious and historical symbol, however, it was an object without peer in Israel's experience. It evoked Moses and the Exodus and the Covenant and a thousand things in Israel's deepest memory. David, then, was anxious to secure it in order to place it in his new capital.

David found the ark at Kirjath Jearim, "the city of woods" (v. 6; 2 Sam. 6:2). Although the Septuagint here calls it "the city of Jearim," that same version does translate the expression in Psalms 131:6 (with reference to the ark) as "the fields of the wood." Even late in the fourth century after Christ, St. Cyril of Jerusalem remarked of the place, "Just a few years ago it was still woody" (*Catechetical Lectures* 12.20).

In this chapter the author begins an implicit contrast of David with Saul. Whereas the ark had been little consulted in Saul's time (v. 3), David will "inquire of" it. Perhaps this is why Michal, Saul's daughter, will scoff at David's devout treatment of the ark (15:29).

Twice in the next chapter we will find David consulting the oracle at the ark of the covenant. Unlike Saul, who "consulted a medium for guidance [but] did not inquire of the LORD" (10:13–14), David will be guided only by God's revelation of His will. The Chronicler returns to this theme in the following chapter.

Though he had no trouble getting the Israelites to agree with his plans for the ark, David found that getting God's cooperation in the project was a tad more complicated. Although he arranged for the most elaborate of processions to bring the ark to Jerusalem (v. 8), the event ended in tragedy because of an unforeseen mishap (vv. 9–10). David's own reaction was a mixture of anger and fear (vv. 11–12).

The interest of the Chronicler here, however, is deeper. He knew that the ark was not being carried in the proper way—that is, by the appointed Levites. The accident occurred on the road because the ark was being carried on a cart drawn by oxen. In the next chapter (15:2), David will see to it that this sort of thing never happens again.

With respect to Uzza, the man who stretched forth his hand to steady the ark so that it would not fall, it will seem to many modern readers that he got a sort of bum rap. After all, his intentions (to the extent that he could be said to have any) were not reprehensible. Generations of commentators have tried to find some moral failing in the man that would explain the severity of his punishment. For example, Josephus (*Antiquities of the Jews* 7.4.2) believed that Uzza died because he was assuming the rights of the priesthood (cf. Num. 4:15; Heb. 5:4).

This is an unnecessary interpretation. There is nothing in the sacred text to suggest a moral failing on Uzza's part. The forgotten premise in such an interpretation of the story is that, according to the Bible, holiness is a very physical thing. And it is also a very dangerous thing. Uzza learned that truth the hard way. Like the Corinthians later on, he died because he failed to "discern" what he was dealing with when he touched the sacred (cf. 1 Cor. 11:27–30).

The things of God are not what we want or understand them to be. God Himself determines what they are, and God has not the slightest concern for our own interpretations of them. Someone approaching the Lord's Supper in an unworthy manner may or may not believe that he is receiving the Body and Blood of the Lord. If he receives that Mystery without faith, however, it is still the Body and Blood of the Lord, and the receiver will partake of damnation. We have God's Word on it.

The holiness is real and objective. It has nothing to do with man's recognition of it. The trespasser who is electrocuted when climbing too high on a high-voltage tower perishes without regard to his own understanding of what he is doing, or his personal theories on electricity, or his perhaps laudable intentions. "And if so much as a beast touches the mountain, it shall be stoned or shot with an arrow" (Heb. 12:20).

1 CHRONICLES 14

THE THREE MONTHS' DELAY in the execution of David's plan (13:14) now permits the author to treat of the geopolitical matters contained in 2 Samuel 5, which he had earlier postponed. From a literary perspective, this arrangement allows the author not only to state explicitly that a certain time period elapsed between David's two attempts to introduce the ark into Jerusalem, but also to fill in those three months with other activity that suggests the passage of time.

The narrative thus provides the chief character, David, some breathing space, as it were, some opportunity, while engaged in other business, to reflect on the tragedy contained in the preceding chapter. Hence, when the Chronicler again turns our attention to the ark in the next chapter, we find David gifted with a new and important insight about the meaning of that tragedy (15:12–13).

The reference to David's multiple wives (v. 3) is the one place in Chronicles which may reflect badly on the king, but even here the author omits the reference to David's concubines in 2 Samuel 5:13. Although he also excises David's adulterous affair with Bathsheba, he does here include a reference to Solomon, Bathsheba's son (v. 4). Given the importance of Solomon to this whole history, the Chronicler could hardly fail to take note of him!

In Josephus (*Antiq.* 7.4.1) the attack of the Philistines described in verses 8–12 is expanded into an international coalition of enemies, which (in spite of the testimony of vv. 1–2) included the Phoenicians. It is more likely the case that David's defeat of the Philistines, who were part of a larger body of European invaders (from Crete and Greece) known in antiquity as "the Sea Peoples," proved to be beneficial to the mercantile aspirations of the Phoenicians. Only with David's defeat of the Sea Peoples did Phoenicia rise again to become a great mercantile power. That is to say, David was every bit as helpful to Hiram king of Tyre as the latter was to him. The defeat of these enemies led to an international recognition of David's stature and prestige (v. 17).

It is clear that the Chronicler has in mind to suggest a contrast between Saul and David. He does this by contrasting the battle of Gilboa (10:1) with the battle of Baal Perazim (vv. 11–12). In the latter case David took care to "inquire of" the Lord (*darash*, v. 14), whereas Saul, who had not inquired of the Lord, inquired of a medium instead (10:13, 14). Indeed, apparently it was Saul who had put a stop to inquiring of the Lord (13:3). Josephus perceived this contrast, remarking that David "never permitted himself to do anything without prophecy and the command of God, and without depending on Him as a safeguard for the future" (*Antiq.* 7.4.1).

Adhering closely to the narrative in 2 Samuel 5:17–25, the Chronicler speaks of a second victory over the Philistines (vv. 13–16).

1 CHRONICLES 15

To HOUSE THE ARK OF THE COVENANT, David provides a tent, presumably on the model of the tabernacle that Moses constructed in the desert (Num. 1:50). When the ark was brought to Jerusalem this time, it was borne on the shoulders of the Levites (vv. 2, 15), as Moses directed (Num. 4:2, 15; Deut. 10:8; 31:25; 1 Sam. 6:15). From now on, David insists, there are to be no mistakes on such matters (v. 13).

David perceived what must be perceived by any who would approach God in worship—God determines the nature, structure, and spirit of the worship. Correct ("orthodox") worship is not the uninformed, spontaneous outpouring of human activity, and the worshipper must be on guard against identifying his own impulses with the agency of the Holy Spirit. Undisciplined, uninformed people are far more likely to act under the impulse of suspect and impure spirits than under the guidance of the Holy Spirit. Mere spontaneity and a "sense of fulfillment" are no adequate indications of the agency of the Holy Spirit.

The Chronicler's introduction of a different subject hints that some time was needed for David to arrive at the perception of this truth. Whereas in 2 Samuel 6:12, David's motive in again attempting to move the ark was a response to the blessings poured out on the family of Obed-Edom, himself a Levite (16:5, 38; Josephus, *Antiq.* 7.4.2), here in Chronicles David is credited with a deeper perception. He perceived that the real problem was the people's relative nonchalance and carelessness in the proper conduct of worship (vv. 12–13). He discerned that in worship it is God who measures man, not the other way round.

David perceived that correct worship is not directly and immediately concerned with the religious needs and aspirations of human beings, but with the glory of God, which is inseparable from His holiness. The fundamental ground of true worship is not the religious nature of man, but the manifestation of God. Indeed, any worship that is not a response to God's Self-revelation must of necessity be idolatrous, the worship of something that man himself creates from the resources of his own religious nature.

For worship to be authentic and true, God Himself must take the initiative. God must be revealed in order for man to worship correctly. Otherwise, man is simply worshipping the works of his own hands, the ideas of his own imagination and reason.

Two chapters earlier, the divine revelation was of a particularly disturbing kind, resulting in a man's death, but it was a true revelation nonetheless, and David properly regarded it as such. He perceived that correct worship does not consist in the attempt to express man's religious aspirations, but in meeting, in faith, the manifestation of God in His truth. David concluded, therefore, that from now on everything would be done decently and in order, as determined in the rules the Lord had given to Moses on the mountain.

This principle pertained first of all to the proper arrangement of the sacred music (v. 16), a matter about which David, himself a musician, took special care. This included instrumental music as well as vocal. This entire section on music (vv. 15–24) we owe to the Chronicler.

The references to "Alamoth" and "Sheminith" (vv. 20–21) may indicate the high (soprano) chords of the harp and the low (baritone) chords of the lyre. The Hebrew word translated as "music" (v. 22) literally means a "burden." This sense is suggested even by the expression "to *lift* the voice" and the idiom "to *carry* a tune." There will be more about this in chapter 25.

"All Israel" (v. 38) brought the ark to the resting place (Ps. 131[132]:8, 14). Once it became clear to this whole assembly—the catholicity of Israel at worship—that the Lord, not man, determines the proper structure and spirit of man's worship, then the Lord assisted and strengthened the worshippers (v. 26, a detail not found in 2 Samuel).

David himself supervised the worship and took an energetic role in its execution (vv. 27, 29).

Michal's scorn of the worship (v. 29) is contrasted with the enthusiasm of the others, especially the Levites, priests, and singers. Continuing the Chronicler's contrast between Saul and David, Michal represents the family of Saul, who had failed to "inquire of" the Lord at the ark.

1 CHRONICLES 16

⚜

THE FIRST THREE AND THE FINAL VERSES OF THIS CHAPTER are the only parts paralleled in 2 Samuel. Josephus himself has none of the material in this chapter.

The psalms appointed for this inaugural celebration of the ark, sometimes referred to in modern scholarship as "the Enthronement of the Lord," correspond very closely to texts contained in the Book of Psalms. Thus, verses 8–22 are substantially identical to Psalm 104[105]:1–15, verses 23–34 to Psalm 95[96]:1–13, and verses 35–36 to Psalm 105[106]:47–48.

Indeed, verse 36 corresponds to the closing verse of Book 4 of the Psalter. If we were to take this verse apart from that context, forgetting its earlier history in the Book of Psalms, we would imagine that the Babylonian Exile preceded the reign of Solomon!

The title of Psalm 95 (96), which ascribes its composition to David himself, records that it was also used at the dedication of the second temple "after the Captivity." The Chronicler appreciated the significance of its also having been sung at the ark's first appearance in Jerusalem more than a half-millennium earlier.

In verse 4 we observe three kinds of prayer: invocation, thanksgiving, and praise.

David's offering of the sacrifices (v. 2) should be understood in the same sense as his constructing of the ritual tent. That is to say, he *caused* these things to be done by others (v. 1; cf. 15:26). David no more "sacrificed" in the sense of taking the place of the priest than he "built" his house in the sense of grabbing the chisel to replace the stonemason or the adze to stand in for the carpenter.

The tent at Jerusalem is distinguished from the one at Gibeon (v. 39), which was instituted by Moses (21:29). It is clear from 1 Kings 3 that the shrine at Gibeon continued to be held in high regard in Israel. This means that for a while Israel had two centers of national worship, and after the translation of the ark to Jerusalem David took care that the regular sacrifices were still to be offered at Gibeon, along with the sacred chants (vv. 40–42). It was at Gibeon that Solomon would have recourse to the Lord at the beginning of his reign.

1 CHRONICLES 17

᪥

IN THE VIEW OF THE CHRONICLER, the temple was supremely David's idea. Whereas in 1 Kings its construction is ascribed to Solomon as the fulfillment of a prophecy made to David, in Chronicles Solomon's role is reduced to carrying out David's own detailed plans.

This view of David's place in the planning of the temple was fixed in Israel's memory by the insertion of Psalm 131 (132) near the end of the Psalms of Ascent, that section of the Psalter (Ps. 119–133 [120–134]) chanted by the pilgrims as they climbed Mount Zion to worship in the temple on the high holy days. In this psalm they called to mind how the construction of God's house had been David's idea. Indeed, Solomon is not so much as named in this psalm. Thus, there is a close historical link between this psalm and the theology of the Chronicler.

This present chapter of Chronicles, which is profitably supplemented with 2 Samuel 7, Psalm 88 (89), and Josephus (*Antiq.* 7.4.4), describes how those plans of David were delayed.

In this scene David wants to build a house (*bayith*) for the Lord, but in fact God also intends to build a house (*bayith*) for David (v. 10)—that is, the lineage of the royal family that will form the Davidic dynasty (v. 12). Only then will there be built a house for the Lord (v. 13). David's own heir will be established in the Lord's house (v. 14). In his prayer of response to this oracle of Nathan, David again refers to his own house in the context of that promise (vv. 16–17, 23–25, 27).

Thus, the "house of the Lord," which is the temple, and the "house of David," which is the Davidic throne, are united by an indissoluble theology. We observe how the Chronicler changes "your house and your kingdom" (2 Sam. 7:16) to "My house and My kingdom" (v. 14). God is Lord of it all, and the distinction between David's house and the Lord's virtually disappears.

The Christian reader will see in this association of God and David an allegory and prophecy of the Incarnation itself, that union of divinity and humanity in a single dwelling place, which is the very flesh of the One of whom the Apostle Paul wrote, "in Him dwells all the fullness of the Godhead bodily" (Col. 2:9).

David, in the prayer that he offers in response to this promise, is said to "sit" before the Lord (v. 16; 2 Sam. 7:18). Since this is the only place in the Hebrew Scriptures when someone is said to sit in prayer, it is not surprising that Josephus (*loc. cit.*) changes the verb to "prostrate." The uniqueness of this case, however, suggests that the act was symbolic, perhaps suggesting a sense of rest in God's presence, of acquiescence in God's decision.

It is also possible that this verb was chosen to parallel the Lord's own "rest" in the temple that David will design. Thus the psalm we cited earlier: "Arise, O LORD, to Your resting place, You and the ark of Your strength. . . . This *is* My resting place forever" (Ps. 131[132]:8, 14). Later on here in 1 Chronicles (28:2), David will use the same Hebrew word for "resting place" (*menuhah*) that we find in this psalm: "I *had* it in my heart to build a house of rest [*beth menuhah*] for the ark of the covenant of the LORD."

Later on, the Chronicler will tell us that the reason David was prohibited from actually building the temple was all the blood he had shed as a warrior (22:8; 28:3). In order to warrant that explanation of the matter, the author proceeds, in this next chapter, to describe David's military exploits.

1 CHRONICLES 18

THESE NEXT THREE CHAPTERS ARE DEVOTED to David's military campaigns. First comes a mention of his conquest of the Philistines (v. 1), already narrated in detail in 14:9–16. Next are the Moabites (v. 2), whose defeat is told here less graphically than in 1 Samuel 22:3. Moving north, David defeats the Zobahites (v. 3) and the Syrians (v. 5). Subjecting all of these nations to his authority, David really did rule eastward to the Euphrates.

Much of this material, with variations, was available to the Chronicler from 2 Samuel 18:1–14, but not the detail about the bronze shields from Syria. It is entirely consistent with the Chronicler's interest in Israel's worship that he should write of Solomon's use of this bronze in the appointments of the temple (v. 8).

Turning south, David conquered the Edomites (vv. 12–13), gaining thereby a port on the Gulf of Aqaba, opening onto the Red Sea and beyond. In due course Solomon will exploit that seaway for vast commercial ventures.

With respect to the slaying of all those Edomites in verse 12, it must be said that several men seem to have been credited with the feat. Here it is ascribed to Abishai, whereas in Psalm 60[59]:1 it is said of Joab, and in 2 Samuel 8:13 David gets the credit.

With respect to David's "court," three items are worth mentioning: First, the "Shavsha" who serves as secretary in verse 16 is called "Seriah" in 2 Samuel and "Seisan" by Josephus. Second, the Cherethites and Pelethites in verse 17 are mercenaries in David's employ. The Cherethites are Cretans, and Pelethites is another name for Philistines.

Third, with respect to David's sons, whom that same verse calls "chief ministers at the king's side," there is also some confusion. 2 Samuel 8:18 says they were "priests," while Josephus (*Antiq.* 7.5.4) makes them "bodyguards." Perhaps various of them functioned in various ways at various times, though it is difficult to understand how they could have been priests, since they were of the tribe of Judah, "of which tribe Moses spoke nothing concerning priesthood" (Heb. 7:14). It may also be the case, one suspects, that the biblical writers simply never could agree on just what David's sons might be good for! Indeed, eventually David had to appoint two other men just to keep an eye on them (27:32).

1 CHRONICLES 19

❦

FOLLOWING THE SEQUENCE IN 2 SAMUEL 9, we would expect David's kind treatment of Mephibosheth to be the next subject. The Chronicler does not tell this story, however, apparently because he wants to forget all about the house of Saul. As far as the Chronicler is concerned, they are all dead (cf. 10:6).

The Ammonite kings, pretty slow learners it would seem, demonstrated a consistent penchant for bad decisions. It was this same Nahash, we recall, whose rash treatment of Jabesh-Gilead provoked the crisis that brought Saul to power more than twenty years earlier (1 Sam. 11). Now, Nahash having died (repentant), his son also acted irresponsibly, incurring the wrath of David (vv. 1–5). The provocation described here differs only slightly from the account in 2 Samuel 10:1–9.

Even before David had time to react, the Ammonites began to prepare for war. This was not David's first time to be thus provoked by a stupid man. One recalls his prompt wrath at an earlier incident when the churlish Nabal treated David's emissaries with disdain (1 Sam. 25).

The ensuing wars against the Ammonites provided the occasion (the siege of Rabbah in the next chapter) on which David and Joab conspired to murder Uriah the Hittite, but we have already noticed that the Chronicler tends to keep his work innocent of such unedifying behavior on David's part.

The descriptions of David's campaign, both here and in 2 Samuel 10, are fairly straightforward and without comment of a religious nature. In neither account, in fact, is God so much as mentioned except by Joab (v. 13; 2 Sam. 10:12). In the story as told by Josephus, however, there is the moral/theological reflection, "But David was not bothered by this alliance, nor disturbed at the might of the Ammonites, but he put his trust in God, conscious of battling for a just cause" (*Antiq.* 7.6.2).

David, after defeating Hanun, appointed the latter's brother Shobi to replace him (2 Sam. 17:27). This detail suggests the breadth of David's recognized power in the region.

1 CHRONICLES 20

⊰

THIS CHAPTER, WHICH TREATS MAINLY OF TROUBLE with the Philistines, begins by completing the Chronicler's treatment of the Ammonites.

In verse 2 the expression "their king" (*malkom*) should probably be read as "Milkom," who was the major Ammonite god (cf. 1 Kings 11:5). (The error in the text here doubtless occurred when later copyists inserted the wrong vowel marks into the text.) This suggested textual emendation of the Hebrew text is bolstered by the Septuagint, which gives the equivalent Greek name, "Molchol" (known elsewhere as Moloch).

Between verses 3 and 4, the Chronicler skips over the entire story of Amnon and Absalom and the rebellion, all the material in 2 Samuel 13:1—21:17. Thus, the great complex drama that fills about one-third of 2 Samuel has no counterpart in Chronicles. Try to imagine a biography of Lincoln that failed to mention the War Between the States!

Sparing the reader that entire scandalous episode, the Chronicler continues in verse 4, which corresponds to 2 Samuel 21:18.

The Chronicler's omission here, explained simply by the fact that the material in question lay outside his interest and perspective, is nonetheless instructive about the variety of historiographies we find in Holy Scripture. Not only is this undeniable variety of perspective compatible with the ascription of divine revelation to the Bible. There is a sense in which the Holy Spirit's authorship of the Scriptures encourages, perhaps even requires, such diversity. That is to say, this variety of historical perspectives indicates the richness, the fruitfulness, of the divine revelation of biblical history.

God's revelation of Himself, we Christians believe, did not take place solely in the inspiration of the Bible, but also in those events that the Bible records. The entire process—history becoming historiography—bears the character of divine revelation.

This consideration prompts another, this one having to do with the historical nature of biblical historiography itself. The divine inspiration of the sacred text does not mean that the biblical historiographer views his subject from a detached, timeless perspective. On the contrary, each biblical historian (including the authors of the four Gospels, for instance), in his treatment of earlier times, embodied also the concerns and perspectives of his own times. What we find in the Bible, then, is a progression in which history interprets history.

In turn, the Bible *creates* history, in the sense that its own interpretations of history serve to influence the history yet to come. Divine revelation is inserted into the world by this ongoing conversation between human history and the sacred book that serves the Church to understand history.

Just as the Bible itself bears witness to a variety of interpretations of biblical history, so the Bible encourages a certain diversity of biblical interpretation, as long as all such interpretations correspond to what the Fathers of the Church called the Rule of Faith. Thus, St. Augustine, in his long treatment of biblical history, wrote, "Now any one may object to this interpretation, and may give another which harmonizes with the Rule of Faith. . . . Although different interpretations are given, yet they must all agree with the one harmonious catholic faith" (*The City of God* 15.26).

1 CHRONICLES 21

ॐ

WITH THEIR NEARLY IDENTICAL STORIES OF THE CENSUS, we perceive a great difference between the Chronicler and the author of Samuel. Whereas in 2 Samuel 24 the account of the census appears to be set apart, as it were, and treated outside the sequence of the narrative, the Chronicler puts it right here in the middle of David's career.

This difference is only apparent, however. In Chronicles the story only *seems* to come earlier in the reign of David, because the Chronicler, as we just saw, has skipped so much of that reign. On the other hand, in these next nine chapters he will include a great deal of material that is *not* found in 2 Samuel, material that relates entirely to David's plan for the coming temple.

Comparing this chapter with its parallel in 2 Samuel 24, we note the Chronicler's inclusion of angelic powers, both the evil angel "Satan" and the remark about the angel of the pestilence (v. 20).

The Chronicler thus ascribes David's temptation to "Satan" (v. 1), a demonic figure with whom the Jews became familiar during the Babylonian Captivity and the Persian period. This "Shatan" is well documented in Zoroastrian literature of that time, and he appears in the postexilic books of Job and Zechariah. The name means "adversary," as in Numbers 22:22. In due course Satan will be recognized as identical with the serpentine tempter who seduced our first parents (cf. Wisdom 2:24; John 8:44; Rev. 12:9; 20:2).

As an expression of David's pride, ambition, and hubris, the census is regarded by both 2 Samuel and 1 Chronicles as something less than his finest hour. Even Joab, hardly a moral giant, recognizes that something is not quite right about it (vv. 3, 6; compare 2 Sam. 24:3).

With respect to the census itself, we observe that the tribe of Levi is not included. This exclusion may have to do with the purpose of the census, which was to provide a "database" for Israel's military conscription. Members of the tribe of Levi were not subject to that conscription.

Benjamin's exclusion evidently had to do with the fact that the census was not completed, because of the plague that came as a punishment.

The story of this plague, here as in 2 Samuel, leads directly to the site of the future temple (vv. 18–27). This is the point that is of greatest interest to the Chronicler. As we have noted, this interest in the "Father's house" provides the basis for the Chronicler's entire history.

The Chronicler alone identifies the site of the future temple as the place where Abraham went to offer Isaac in sacrifice (v. 18; 2 Chr. 3:1; Gen. 22:2). We shall later reflect on this very important identification.

1 CHRONICLES 22

꙼

IN 2 SAMUEL 24:30 THE PLAGUE STORY is followed immediately by David's old age and death, but here in Chronicles David is just getting started! Yet we are dealing with exactly the same time frame as in 2 Samuel. David's real and best work, for the Chronicler, still lies ahead—namely, the temple. He promptly begins to assemble the material for this great enterprise (vv. 2–3).

Because in the Bible's prophetic view this temple was to be a "house of prayer for all nations" (Mark 11:17), it is theologically significant that the Gentiles participated in its construction (v. 2). Of course they will also be involved in the building of the second temple (Is. 60:10). Here in this fleeting reference in Chronicles, then, lies hidden the mystery that Paul will explore in Romans 9—11, the engrafting of the Gentiles onto the stock of Israel.

Solomon is still young (v. 5); we can only guess how old he was at his accession. Not even the Jews could agree; Josephus estimated that Solomon was fourteen, and Rashi said twelve. First Kings, on the other hand, seems to make him fully an adult. In any case, David gives the young man proper instruction with respect to the temple (vv. 7–16). As Moses passed on to his successor Joshua the authority to conquer the Promised Land, so David here authorizes his successor to build the Lord's house. In 2 Timothy there will once again be the sense of such a transition, as Paul, preparing to die, hands on to Timothy the historical ministry of the Church.

In verse 9 there is a play on various words having to do with "peace" (*shalom*). Solomon's name, Shlomo, means "his peace," and Shalem is an ancient variant for Jerusalem. This emphasis on peace in David's last exhortation to Solomon stands in sharp contrast to the final instructions about blood-vengeance that David gives to Solomon in 1 Kings.

Indeed, the fact that David had shed much blood was the reason given for his inability to see the temple's construction through to the end (v. 6; 28:3). The temple would always be more associated with Solomon, whose very name suggests peace. The Chronicler is sensitive to this point. War, even justified war, even necessary war, yet carries a quality of defilement incompatible with the proper worship of God. Men are to offer their prayers with "holy hands, without wrath" (1 Tim. 2:8). Blood, in the Bible, is a holy thing. To have shed blood in anger—which in warfare takes place in profusion—carries a ritual, if not a moral, defilement that fits ill with the purity of God's worship. This persuasion has always been expressed in the Church's canons on priestly ordination.

1 CHRONICLES 23

THIS CHAPTER BEGINS BY ELABORATING THE SCENE in 1 Kings 1 into the full-blown co-regency, as it were, of Solomon with David (v. 1).

Then comes a long section on the Levites. The Chronicler, after telling us (in 21:6) that the Levites were not counted, now proceeds to give us a detailed count of them (vv. 2–24).

The description of the work of the Levites makes it clear that their ministry was subordinate and ancillary to that of the priests (vv. 24–32). They cared for the music and many other tasks associated with the worship but did not, it appears, perform the sacrifices central to the temple's ritual. Consequently, it is not surprising that the Christian Church, from before the end of the first century, has thought of the order of Levites as the Old Testament's parallel to the New Testament diaconate (Clement of Rome, *Corinthians* 40.5).

The outstanding quality of the liturgy in the temple may be gauged by the fact that it was accompanied by an orchestra of four thousand (v. 5)! (With respect to David's interest in musical instruments, see 7:6; 29:26; Neh. 12:36; Josephus, *Antiq.* 7.12.3.) This figure suggests massive, continuous praise (v. 6).

In verse 30 we find early evidence for the beginning of those two major hours of daily Christian prayer. The times of the morning and evening sacrifices in the temple became the times of daily prayer in the synagogue, and these services passed directly into the Christian Church as Matins and Vespers, which abide to the present day. Both of these daily offices of Christian worship are the historical extensions of the services described in this chapter of Chronicles.

Verses 21–22 demonstrate the common biblical meaning of the expression "brethren," or "brothers and sisters." In these verses it is logically impossible for the young ladies, who are described as having no brothers, to marry their brothers, if we depend on the standard English use of those terms. Clearly these women are marrying their cousins, for which there is no special word in either Hebrew or Aramaic. In Holy Scripture the expression "brothers and sisters" only rarely corresponds to the meaning of that same expression in common English.

This usage must be borne in mind when we read about the "brothers and sisters" of Jesus in the New Testament. The expression is properly interpreted in accord with the traditional view, held by the entire Christian tradition without exception (including the Protestant Reformers of the sixteenth century), that the Mother of Jesus, whose very body was consecrated by the Divine Son's becoming incarnate in her womb, remained a virgin all her life.

1 CHRONICLES 24

ঔৄ

THE CHRONICLER NOW RUNS THROUGH THE COURSES of the priests, who took their turns at the various liturgical functions in the sanctuary (vv. 1–19). There "the priests always went into the first part of the tabernacle, performing *the services*" (Heb. 9:6). There they stood, "ministering daily and offering repeatedly the same sacrifices, which can never take away sins" (Heb. 10:11).

One of the most memorable portraits of the Old Testament priest leading the worship of the temple comes from the pen of Ben Sirach, who described Simon the high priest in the second century before Christ:

When he went up to the holy altar, lending honor to the vestment of holiness. And when he took the portions out of the hands of the priests, he himself stood by the altar, while about him was ranged the ring of his brethren: and as the cedar planted in Mount Lebanon, like as branches of palm trees, they encircled him, all the sons of Aaron in their glory. And the oblation of the Lord was in their hands, in the presence of all the congregation of Israel. Completing his service at the altar, to honor the offering of this exalted circle, he extended his hand to pour out a libation and to offer of the blood of the grape. He poured out at the foot of the altar a divine odor to the Most High Prince. Then the sons of Aaron shouted; they sounded with beaten trumpets and were loud with acclaim to be heard for a remembrance before God. Then all the people hastened together and fell down to the earth upon their faces, adoring the Lord their God and praying to Almighty God, the most High. The singers lifted up their voices, and in the great house there swelled forth sound of sweet melody. And the people in prayer besought the Lord the most High, until the worship of the Lord was brought to perfection, and they had finished their service. Then coming down, he lifted up his hands over all the congregation of the children of Israel, to give glory to God with his lips and to glory in his name: And he repeated his prayer, fervent to show forth the power of God (Ecclus. 50:12–23, author's translation).

All this worship was symbolic of the liturgy of heaven, where the true High Priest, Jesus the Lord, "entered the Most Holy Place once for all, having obtained eternal redemption" (Heb. 9:12). Accordingly, the twenty-four courses of the priests in this chapter of 1 Chronicles correspond to the heavenly sanctuary's twenty-four elders, who worship day and night before the Throne (Rev. 4:4, 10), offering the prayers of the saints (5:8).

Particularly to be noted in this list is the eighth course, that of Abijah (v. 10). In due time one of the priests of Abijah's course, Zacharias (Luke 1:5), would draw the lot to offer incense in the sanctuary (Luke 1:8–9). The beginning of all good things, this scene opens the Gospel of Luke.

This list of the twenty-four courses of the priesthood will be paralleled in the next chapter by twenty-four groups of temple singers (25:31).

In the present chapter the list of the priestly courses is followed by another listing of Levites. No one has adequately explained to the present writer why this second list of Levites, which contains ten names not found in the previous chapter, has been inserted at this unexpected place.

1 CHRONICLES 25

꙾

MORE THAN ONE COMMENTATOR ON HOLY SCRIPTURE, observing the Chronicler's partiality toward the Levitical singers (15:16–22; 16:4–42; 2 Chr. 15:12–13; 29:27–30; cf. Ezra 3:10; Neh. 12:27), has suggested that the Chronicler himself may have been numbered among them.

Corresponding to the twenty-four courses of the officiating priests, the Chronicler now introduces us to an equal number of groups of temple musicians.

Particularly to be noted in this chapter is the ease with which the Chronicler associates music with prophecy. Thus, the musicians are said to "prophesy with harps, stringed instruments, and cymbals" (v. 1), and the author speaks of "their father Jeduthun, who prophesied with a harp to give thanks and to praise the Lord" (v. 3).

Earlier, in chapter 15, we observed that the very expression "to lift up the voice" suggested that music was a "burden" of some kind. Indeed, the word employed there, *massa'*, which comes from the root *ms'* ("to lift"), also means "oracle." So often in the prophetic writings we find the expression "the *burden* of the Lord" in the sense of a prophetic statement.

No one in antiquity questioned the relationship between prophecy and music, not even Saul (cf. 1 Sam. 10:5). It was not unknown, "when the musician played, that the hand of the LORD came upon him" (2 Kings 3:15). In the Bible one moves easily from the prophets to the psalms (cf. Luke 24:44), and the Bible's chief musician, David, is also called a prophet.

David's own place in the history of Israel's liturgical music was so dominant in the tradition that it became customary among the Church Fathers to ascribe to him the authorship of whatever parts of the Psalter were not otherwise ascribed. David's name became synonymous with the Book of Psalms very much as Solomon's with Proverbs and Moses' with the Pentateuch.

The present chapter should remind us that the singing of hymns is a normal and essential part of the Christian's birthright. Indeed, the chanting of psalms, hymns, and spiritual canticles is an essential, irreplaceable feature of the Church's worship of God. This feature is, if anything, even more characteristic of the Church in glory (cf. Rev. 4:8–11; 5:8–14; and so on).

1 CHRONICLES 26

⌘

THE OFFICE OF PORTER, OR GATEKEEPER (vv. 1–19), was not so humble and insignificant as the name may suggest. These men, in fact, enjoyed considerable prestige as ministers of the sanctuary, serving in such functions as did not require the ministry of a priest.

Indeed, for many centuries and differing somewhat from place to place, the Christian Church revived this ministry as one of the minor orders and graced it with a rite of ordination. Analogous to the porters of the Old Testament, these Christian porters were charged with such responsibilities as the locking and unlocking of the church doors (hence their name, from the Latin word for door, *porta*), the ringing of the bells for the sacred services (and therefore care of the church clocks), the maintenance of certain material elements used in those services (such as prayer books and hymnals), and the general upkeep of the sanctuary.

With all the candles and incense consumed by fire, vestments soiled, oil inadvertently spilt, penitential ashes accidentally dispersed, bay leaves and rose petals scattered for special feasts, and so forth, it is no small work to keep a church building clean.

As these duties were gradually taken over by others (which would always be the case in those congregations that did not have an ordained porter), the Christian order of porter eventually disappeared. (The Roman Catholic Church, for instance, stopped ordaining porters in the early 1970s.) Even if they are no longer ordained, a special respect and honor is due to those who take care of a church building, mend its vestments and linens, polish its candlesticks, maintain the appointments of its worship, clean its floors and windows, arrange its flowers, dust its pews, replace its light bulbs, and adorn it for the special services of feast days. These folks, the spiritual progeny of those who cared for the temple of David and Solomon, are especially respected in that temple made without hands.

We have already reflected that the higher office of Levite in the Old Testament became the model for the office of deacon in the Christian Church. In particular, we may note that Christian deacons, like the

Jewish Levites (vv. 20, 24, 26–28), have traditionally been charged with the oversight of the Church's material resources, becoming the successors to those original seven who served at tables in the early Church (Acts 6).

As they managed the physical and financial assets of the Church, it often happened that deacons became very powerful. In some places it was not unusual for a deacon to succeed the bishop he served. Among the more famous deacons who did so was St. Athanasius of Alexandria in the fourth century.

1 CHRONICLES 27

୬ଡ଼

NEITHER LIST IN THIS CHAPTER has a parallel in 2 Samuel.

The first list (vv. 1–15) is similar to the earlier list of David's heroes (11:11–47), but it is not derivative from it. Unlike the lists of the preceding chapter, it identifies, not the ministers of the sanctuary, but those individuals and households who regularly ("month by month") provided King David with the material means of constructing the temple. These are called "the heads of fathers' *houses*" and "captains" (v. 1).

Corresponding to the twelve months of the year and the traditional number of twelve tribes, these are divided into twelve taxation districts (vv. 25–31), an arrangement that would continue under Solomon (1 Kings 4).

The constant repetition of their numbers as "twenty-four thousand" corresponds to the division of the priests into twenty-four courses of ministerial rotation, which we considered earlier. This number is also surely related to the twenty-four elders we find around God's throne in Revelation 4.

Thus, in the constantly repeated "twenty-four thousand" we should detect the influence of a sacral and hierarchical interest in the list. Two things should be borne in mind regarding the historicity of these figures. First, as we have seen before, the word *'eleph*, translated as "thousand," was a technical rather than a strictly mathematical reference. Second, it would require a truly unusual miracle to guarantee that each district would have exactly the same number of male adults at exactly the same time.

This chapter's second list (vv. 16–22) names Israel's tribal leaders during David's reign, indicating the king's apparent comfort with the continuance of the ancient tribal leadership. This was to be less the case during the reign of Solomon. In fact, a festering discord between Solomon's style of rule and the traditional tribal authority was to contribute greatly to the schism that ensued on Solomon's death.

The chapter contains a note on David's refusal to permit the results of his census to be entered into the archives of the realm (vv. 23–24), since that census offended God and was regarded as a blight on David's reign. It does appear, therefore, that both the Chronicler and the author of 2 Samuel received the results of that census from other sources. This would in part explain why they are somewhat different.

The chapter's final section (vv. 25–34) indicates that the king's property, a major source of the revenue by which the governing was done, grew during David's reign. It is a simple fact, after all, that the needs of government tend to grow. If this development continued during the reigns of subsequent kings—as surely it did—a certain resentment was bound to be the result. It is instructive to observe that Ezekiel, writing over four centuries after David, preferred that the royal properties be strictly fixed (Ezek. 46:16–18).

1 CHRONICLES 28

DAVID DID NOT SIMPLY ABDICATE THE THRONE in favor of Solomon; he placed that succession, rather, in a larger framework of tradition, so that his son would benefit from the support and counsel of "all the leaders of Israel: the officers of the tribes and the captains of the divisions" (v. 1). The king was the representative of the whole nation, and his accession to the throne was inseparable from that representation.

Basing his work on this high calling of Israel's kings, the Chronicler omits from his succession narrative the dramatic and often chaotic intrigues among David's ambitious sons, stories that fill eight chapters between 2 Samuel 13 and 1 Kings 2. For the Chronicler these events are simply not significant. Those shallow, ephemeral incidents are petty and uninteresting. They do not even begin to touch the true meaning of Solomon's accession to the throne.

In the Chronicler's account of the matter, David simply announces that God picked Solomon, and that settles the matter of the transition (v. 5). Solomon, whom the Lord hereby adopts as His son, will build the temple (v. 6) that David was unable to complete (v. 3).

We observe, in this matter of succession, that Solomon is not David's oldest son, but neither was David the oldest son of Jesse (v. 4). In fact, from the day the Lord's choice fell on Seth rather than Cain, He has shown scant regard for the human tradition of primogeniture. God's choices have nothing to do with man's calculations.

Drawing the blueprint of the temple is ascribed to David (vv. 11–12), just as transmitting the blueprint of the desert tabernacle was ascribed to Moses (Ex. 25:9; Heb. 9:1–2), and as the mystic Ezekiel will provide the blueprint for the second temple. In each instance, the design is "revealed"; that is, it is known "by the Spirit" (*baruach*, v. 12; cf. v. 19). Such constructions are modeled on the heavenly sanctuary, which Moses beheld on the mountain and which John gazed upon in the mystic visions of Patmos (cf. Heb. 8:5; 9:1–5). Man's entire endeavor to worship God is an attempt to create on earth an image of heaven.

The history of God's people, then, is a chronicle of temple building. Indeed, the construction of a dwelling place for the Lord—the mystery of the temple—is the very goal of history. Such is the perspective of the Chronicler, who uses this viewpoint to distinguish between what is truly important and what is not. This is his interpretive lens through which to survey the course of years and centuries. It is a narrative wisdom higher and more serene.

Although David has already given this charge to Solomon in private (22:6–16), he now does so in the sight of "all Israel" (v. 4). This charge contains what the Chronicler regards as the true substance of orthodox historical transmission—namely, provision for the orthodox worship of God. Solomon's duties include, therefore, not only the construction of the temple but also the oversight of its worship.

For the Chronicler, then, Israel's anointed kingship is directly related to Israel's worship, for it is the king who provides the priests and Levites and supplies their needs. This is how the king must justify his existence, and such is the standard by which the Chronicler will now begin to assess the reign of each monarch that inherits David's throne.

1 CHRONICLES 29

᠅

IT IS BOTH INTERESTING AND PROFITABLE to compare the instructions David gives Solomon near the end of 1 Chronicles with the instructions this same David gives to this same Solomon in 1 Kings 2:1–9. In the Kings account David commends certain irreproachable moral instructions to Solomon (1 Kings 21:14) and then goes on to recommend the killing of Joab and the punishing of Shimei (21:5–6, 8–9). In the Chronicles account, on the other hand, David goes to great length instructing Solomon with respect to the temple, its priesthood, and its worship. The differences between the two stories are . . . well, striking.

Similarly, here in the Chronicler's narrative of the submission of Solomon's brothers to their new king (v. 24), he leaves out the more colorful account found in 1 Kings 1:5–49. Such details, for the Chronicler, would constitute something of a distraction from his chosen theme.

David, in his final charge to the nation, summons the people to be generous for the construction of the temple (vv. 1–5). His words are modeled on the similar charge that Moses gave to the Israelites with respect to the tabernacle in the wilderness (Ex. 35:4–19).

In describing those ancient events, the Chronicler employs terms characteristic of the Persian period during which he is writing. Thus, one of the terms he uses in reference to the temple is *birah*, a Persian word meaning "palace" (vv. 1, 19). Nowhere else in the Bible is the temple called by that name, though we do find the expression rather often, in its usual and secular sense, in this and other works from the Persian and Greek periods (2 Chr. 17:12; 27:4; Neh. 1:1; 2:8; 7:2; Esther 1:2, 5; 2:3, 5, 8; 3:15; 8:14; 9:6, 11, 12; Dan. 8:2).

In like fashion, the wealth given for the construction of the temple is measured by its equivalent in the golden coins of Persia, the *'adarkanim* ("darics," v. 7). The use of such expressions rendered the Chronicler's story more intelligible to his contemporaries.

The rich theology of the Chronicler is perhaps nowhere more explicit than in David's closing prayer (vv. 10–19), a solemn liturgical blessing that epitomizes God's true worship at all times. At the heart of this prayer is the mystery of the temple. It is prayer, after all, that makes a temple a temple, and David's blessing here contains the sentiments of humility of that other man who, having prayed in the temple with humility, went down to his house more justified than the other (v. 14; Luke 18:9–14).

The Chronicler names three literary sources for his description of the reign of David (v. 29). The only one of these three sources still extant is the Books of Samuel and 1 Kings. The other material found in the Books of Chronicles, we presume, must be attributed to those sources that have not otherwise come down to us.

The major contribution of the Chronicler, as compared with the Books of Samuel, is all the extensive material relative to David's preparation for the temple and its worship. Samuel devotes 77 verses to David's liturgical concerns, whereas here in 1 Chronicles there are 323 verses devoted to this theme.

This difference of Chronicles from the Books of Samuel and Kings is not only material, it is also formal. That is to say, it pertains not only to *what* was written, but also to *why* it was written. The Chronicler had in mind to portray David as a man of worship more than as a political and military figure. In this respect David most resembles Moses.

This view of David is based on the Chronicler's view of biblical history. The history of Israel, for this writer, is the history of worship. It is Israel's worship, therefore, that defines the Chronicler's historical perspective.

2 CHRONICLES 1

AS WE REFLECTED EARLIER, THIS BOOK WAS ORIGINALLY the second half of a single work, known in Hebrew as "the words of the days," meaning "history." Since, however, Hebrew does not, strictly speaking, have vowel letters, the original "Book of Chronicles" was quite a bit shorter in Hebrew than in Greek. Thus, when the work was translated into the latter language in the third century before Christ, the greater number of letters rendered the work too bulky to be transcribed onto a single scroll. Hence, it was divided into two parts, as we have it now. The present work, therefore, is a strict continuation of 1 Chronicles. The transition was originally seamless.

Accordingly, as in David's last public appearance (1 Chr. 28—29), Solomon is surrounded by "all Israel" (v. 2). Describing the new king's pilgrimage to Gibeon, the Chronicler goes into greater detail, including elements not found in Kings (vv. 3b–6a) that emphasize the continuity of Solomon's *novus ordo* with the ancient institutions of Moses.

The new king was expected to make this pilgrimage because of the veneration widely and deeply felt toward the Mosaic tabernacle, now about three hundred years old, and the ancient bronze altar made by Bezalel (Ex. 31; 38). Solomon's pilgrimage to this traditional gathering place of the tribes further signified that the new temple, which he would soon undertake to build, represented no break from Israel's inherited worship.

Josephus, in spite of the combined testimonies of both Kings and Chronicles, places this event at Hebron. He also adds the amusing detail that when the Lord spoke to Solomon—in a dream in Kings but in a vision in Chronicles—the king "jumped out of bed" (*Antiq.* 8.2.1.). Well, yes, I suppose that does make sense.

Solomon, in response to the Lord's offer to give him whatever he wanted (v. 7), requested only spiritual goods, not military conquest or worldly power. He besought the Lord for the wisdom (v. 10) that became the trait for which he is best remembered, both in Holy Scripture and in the minds of believers ever since.

Nonetheless, because Solomon's reign was also a time of economic prosperity, the Chronicler could hardly remain silent about the king's mercantile skills (vv. 14–17). Solomon, then, seeking first the kingdom of God and His righteousness, discovered that all these other things had been added to him as well. Even in this respect, however, the Chronicler, inspired by another view of what is really important in history, omits many of the details about Solomon's wealth found in 1 Kings.

All these matters now being settled, the Chronicler is ready to get to the really important part of the story, the construction of the temple.

2 CHRONICLES 2

☙

SOLOMON'S GREAT BUILDING PROJECT BEGINS.

As though the fact were an afterthought barely mentioned in just two Hebrew words, we are told that Solomon also planned "a royal house for himself" (v. 1; 1:18 in the traditional Hebrew text). This latter construction, which served for governmental administration as well as Solomon's residence, required elaborate planning and labor over a period of thirteen years (1 Kings 7:1–12). Once again, we note, as in the case of David, the Chronicler is relatively uninterested in this political and worldly aspect of Solomon's reign. He all but ignores it. In the eyes of this writer, the historical importance of Solomon had to do entirely with the temple and what took place there.

Writing long after the worldly prestige and power of the Davidic monarchy had disappeared from the geopolitical scene, the Chronicler was not disposed to dwell on the worldly grandeur of Solomon's reign. All that greatness was gone. What, then, asked the Chronicler, was Solomon's real historical significance? What was the true, important legacy of his reign? It was the temple, the institutional provision for the worship of God. In this effort lay the genuine greatness of Solomon. This was the authentic work of the wisdom with which the Lord endowed him (v. 12). It was his provision for the worship of God that made Solomon's reign significant.

This significance is expressed in detail and at length in Solomon's letter to Hiram (Huram in the Hebrew), which the Chronicler employs to elaborate the theology the temple will embody. This letter, along with Hiram's response, goes to the heart of the matter.

The temple, first of all, will not "contain" God in the sense of being His adequate residence. Although the Lord's "name" will dwell there (v. 4; cf. 1 Chr. 28:3; 29:16), the house itself is properly intended for man's *worship* of Him (vv. 4b–7, with no parallel in 1 Kings).

God Himself, after all, cannot be enclosed in space. Even the highest heaven, the place of that true tabernacle not made with hands, is unable to contain the One that made it (v. 6). Such was the new king's conviction, and if he had adopted any other attitude toward his work, Solomon's very temple would have become only a more subtle form of worldliness.

The reply of Hiram (especially vv. 11–12) should be read as the Gentiles' proper response to Solomon's plan. In the full context of biblical history and revelation, Hiram and his skilled artisan Huram (v. 13) foreshadow the Magi and all other generations of Gentiles that will come with their gifts to worship the God of David and Solomon. Hiram here plays Cornelius to Solomon's Peter.

Properly to understand this correspondence, then, we should read Solomon's letter rather in the way we read those of the Apostle Paul—as a proclamation of the Gospel to the nations. Hiram's letter, in turn, is the faithful response to that proclamation.

Later on, in the Acts of the Apostles, Luke's long narrative of the apostolic mission to the Gentiles, Stephen's famous sermon on the true significance of the temple will serve as a sort of manifesto. In order to make way for that evangelical extension, Stephen will die for making the same assertion that Solomon makes here in Chronicles (Acts 7:47–50). Solomon's building of the temple, then, an endeavor in which the Gentiles too have their part, foreshadows the mission of the Apostles to construct God's true and universal place of worship in this world.

2 CHRONICLES 3

～ঌ৵

THIS CHAPTER IS THE ONLY PLACE in Holy Scripture where the location of the temple is identified as Mount Moriah (v. 1), the very site where Abraham took Isaac to be sacrificed (Gen. 22:2). This is no incidental detail. By introducing this connection of the temple to that distant event, not only does the Chronicler subtly indicate the new temple's continuity with the distant patriarchal period, but he also provides his readers with a very rich theme of theology.

The ancient scene on Mount Moriah is the Bible's first mention of a "substitutionary sacrifice." Abraham and Isaac, father and son, climb the mountain of immolation (Gen. 22:6). In the enigmatic conversation between the two climbers (Gen. 22:7–8), the attentive Bible-reader perceives a rich mystery concealed in Abraham's reply that "God will provide for Himself the lamb for a burnt offering." The Chronicler's mention of Moriah in the present chapter shows his awareness that Abraham's words are prophetic of the many paschal lambs sacrificed in the temple.

Isaac himself, we recall, said nothing in reply (Gen. 22:9–10). Indeed, Isaac remained entirely silent after Abraham spoke. He was like a lamb led to the slaughter that opens not his mouth (Is. 53:7). In his sacrificial silence, Isaac bore in himself the mystery of the temple and its worship.

We discern this mystery in the victim substituted for Isaac, the ram caught by its horns. This is the Bible's first instance of a substitution made in the matter of sacrifice. This ram caught in the bush foreshadows, first of all, the paschal lamb of the Mosaic Covenant, which would be slaughtered on behalf of Israel's firstborn sons on the night of the Exodus. In Genesis 22, then, we are dealing with the Bible's earliest configuration of a category important in biblical soteriology. The paschal lambs offered in Solomon's temple over the centuries were all prefigured by that earlier event on Mount Moriah. The attentive reader will observe that the Chronicler never mentions a celebration of Passover except in Jerusalem (cf. chs. 30; 35).

The Christian will, of course, perceive this mystery in its true fullness. The Apostle Paul appealed to this category of substitution when he wrote that God "did not spare His own Son, but delivered Him up for us all" (Rom. 8:32). Echoing this text from Romans, Irenaeus of Lyons wrote in the second century, "Abraham, according to his faith, adhered to the command of God's Word, and with a ready mind delivered up, as a sacrifice to God, his only-begotten and beloved son, in order that God also might be pleased to offer up, for all his seed, His own beloved and only-begotten Son, as a sacrifice for our redemption" (*Against the Heresies* 4.5.4).

Hence, Isaac carrying the wood up the sacrificial hill has always signified to Christian readers—at least since a paschal homily of Melito of Sardis in the second century—the willingness of God's own Son, the true Paschal Lamb, to take up the cross and carry it to the place of immolation.

2 CHRONICLES 4

WE COME NOW TO THE FURNISHINGS OF THE TEMPLE. It will have, first of all, a brazen altar, *mizbach nechosheth*, the counterpart of the Mosaic altar at Gibeon (v. 1; 1:6; Ex. 38:30), but larger.

In front of this altar will stand a large basin with a diameter of roughly seventeen feet, calculated to hold ten thousand gallons of water (vv. 2, 5). Indeed, rabbinical commentators believed that the priests, who used it for bathing (v. 6), completely immersed themselves in it. The water in this basin was also dipped out to clean the sacrificial animals (v. 7).

A "sea" this basin was called, a name that Josephus ascribes to the sheer size of the thing (*Antiq.* 8.3.5), but an object so large with so suggestive a name was not long in assuming a more complex symbolism. Solomon's sea seems to symbolize those primeval waters of Creation, over which the Spirit of God hovered at the beginning of Genesis.

These two appointments of the temple, the altar and the sea, both have their counterparts in that heavenly tabernacle made without hands: the golden altar on which are offered the prayers of the saints (Rev. 6:9; 8:3–5; 9:13; 11:1; 14:18; 16:7), and the glassy sea (4:6; 15:2) near which gather the twenty-four ancients that symbolize the twenty-four divisions of the priesthood (4:4; 1 Chr. 24:1–19).

Solomon's ten lampstands will provide the illumination necessary in an area largely cut off from daylight (v. 7; 1 Kings 7:49). Presumably they will be placed on the ten serving tables (v. 8), but this is not certain. Josephus, whom we suspect of getting a bit carried away on the matter, places the number of candlesticks at ten thousand! He further ascribes that high number to an injunction from Moses (*Antiq.* 8.3.7), a point that the present writer does not find so obvious in Holy Scripture.

The aforesaid ten tables will also, it would seem, hold the numerous smaller vessels and implements necessary to the sacrificial ritual (vv. 11, 16, 22).

Only the Chronicler mentions that the showbread was placed on multiple tables (v. 20; 1 Chr. 28:16).

The temple area will be divided into courts, each having its own specific accessibility. The "great court," an outer court, will be available to all that are "distinguished from the rest by being pure and observant of the laws" (Josephus, *Antiq.* 8.3.9), whereas the smaller court will be reserved for priests (v. 9). The later, postexilic temple will be even further divided.

2 CHRONICLES 5

WHILE THE BUILDING OF THE TEMPLE must be credited to Solomon, the Chronicler neglects no opportunity to mention that David had already prepared its inner furnishings, appointments, and sacred vessels (v. 1). These are now to be transported to the new temple with an elaborate procession, which will include a large number of Levitical singers and musicians (v. 12).

These ceremonies took place in Israel's seventh month (v. 3), corresponding to our mid-autumnal season. Since the temple itself would not be completed until a month later (1 Kings 6:38), we surmise that Solomon wanted these various appointments, especially the ark of the covenant, to be in place as early as possible, even before the finishing touches were made on the temple. Indeed, if similar examples from our own times may be invoked to illustrate the setting, it is possible that Solomon intended the events in this chapter to serve as an extra nudge to the temple builders themselves to hustle things up a bit.

Prior to the procession to the temple, the traditional heads and representatives of the tribes assembled at the tabernacle David had constructed in Jerusalem (v. 2), and for the last time sacrifices were offered in that place (v. 6).

Although the Levites removed the ark from the Davidic tabernacle (v. 4), it was the task of the priests to carry it into the inner shrine of the temple, called "the Most Holy Place" (v. 7), which only the priests were permitted to enter.

We should not read this chapter as simply the narrative of the Chronicler, because in some places he seems to be copying out an earlier account, to which his own transcription strives to be faithful. In these cases the Chronicler's story line reflects, not his own period, but that of his earlier source. We have a clear example of this when the Chronicler writes of the ark's carrying handles that "they are there to this day" (v. 9). This latter statement certainly does not refer to the Chronicler's own time, long after Solomon's temple had been destroyed (and replaced), but to the time of the pre-exilic source the Chronicler is quoting.

Respecting the contents of the ark, the Chronicler specifies that it held only the two tablets of the Decalogue (v. 10; Deut. 10:2). This reference, too, reflects a particular period in Israel's history, difficult to identify. We do know that, at least at some time during that history, the ark contained "the golden pot that had the manna, Aaron's rod that budded, and the tablets of the covenant" (Heb. 9:4; cf. Num. 17:25).

The service and procession ended with the outpouring of the cloud of the divine glory, which sanctified the event (vv. 13–14). Josephus (*Antiq.* 8.4.2) describes the experience:

Now as soon as the priests had put all things in order about the ark, and were gone out, there came down a thick cloud, and stood there, and spread itself, after a gentle manner, into the temple; it was a diffused and temperate cloud, not a rough one as we see full of rain in the winter season. This cloud so darkened the place, that one priest could not discern another, but it afforded to the minds of all a visible image and glorious appearance of God's having descended into this temple, and of his having gladly pitched his tabernacle therein.

2 CHRONICLES 6

THE DARKNESS OF THE CLOUD OF THE DIVINE PRESENCE is thematically linked to Solomon's consecratory prayer, which fills this chapter. The temple, this "exalted house" (v. 2) in which God's "name" (vv. 6, 7, 9, 10, 20) dwells forever, is associated with that mysterious cloud by which He guided His people through the passage of the Red Sea and the Desert of Sinai (v. 1). The cloud on Mount Sinai thus becomes the cloud on Mount Zion (cf. Ex. 20:21; Heb. 12:21).

For purposes of analysis, we may divide Solomon's prayer into three major parts, followed by concluding verses.

The first part is a benediction, a blessing of the Lord God of Israel (*baruch Adonai 'Elohei Isra'el*—v. 4), in which the king also "blessed the whole assembly of Israel" (*wayebarek 'eth kol qahal Isra'el*—v. 3). That is to say, Israel is blessed in the act of blessing God. This benediction concentrates on the promise God made to David respecting His "temple" (*bayith*—vv. 7, 9, 10).

This temple, or house, is associated with three covenants. First, there is the covenant with Abraham, already indicated by the temple's construction on the very site of Abraham's sacrifice (3:1), and quietly suggested here by Solomon's reference to the command that ancient patriarch received from the Lord (v. 14; Gen. 17:1). Next, there is the covenant of Mount Sinai, mediated through Moses at the time of the Exodus (v. 5) and enshrined in the ark of the covenant (v. 11). Finally, the temple is associated with the Lord's covenant with David (v. 10).

These latter two covenants are again tied together in the closing lines of the prayer (vv. 41–42), which indicate the indissoluble bond between the ark of the covenant and the throne of David. The Chronicler well knew that both institutions suffered the same fate in the summer of 587, when the Babylonians razed the temple and abolished the monarchy.

The second part of Solomon's prayer, in which he turns toward the altar, kneeling and spreading his arms (vv. 12–13, lines proper to the Chronicler), again invokes the Davidic covenant and pleads for its confirmation (vv. 15–17). Specifically, Solomon prays that the new temple will be a sort of gathering place for all the prayers offered in its direction, from any part of the world (vv. 18–21; Dan. 6:10; 9:19).

In the third section of his prayer (vv. 22–39), Solomon runs through a list of hypothetical situations of distress in which God's servants may at any time find themselves. We may compare Psalm 106[107], with its repeated instances of such prayer, along with its double refrain, "Then they cried out to the LORD in their trouble, / *And* He delivered them out of their distresses," and "Oh, that *men* would give thanks to the LORD *for* His goodness, / And *for* His wonderful works to the children of men!"

2 CHRONICLES 7

҂ఞ

The Lord's fiery response to Solomon's prayer (v. 1) caused those gathered at the temple to fall prostrate in worship and praise (v. 3). One recalls that when the prayer of Elijah brought sacrificial fire from heaven, the response of the onlookers was identical (1 Kings 18:36–39).

The descent of the divine fire to consume the initial sacrifices in the temple is not mentioned except in Chronicles, which also noted the same miracle when David earlier offered sacrifices on that very site, Ornan's threshing floor (1 Chr. 21:26). In Leviticus 9:24 the same miracle sealed the consecration of Aaron.

In pursuit of one of his usual themes, only the Chronicler mentions the musical ministry that accompanied these dedicatory sacrifices in the temple (v. 6).

It seems that this autumnal celebration, which lasted a whole eight days (v. 8), finished on the first day of the Feast of Tabernacles, which also lasted eight days (v. 9; Lev. 23:36). The account in Chronicles thus clarifies an obscurity about the length of the celebration in 1 Kings 8:65–66.

Perhaps it would have been a distraction to the Chronicler to mention that Yom Kippur also fell during the eight days of the temple's dedication (cf. Num. 29:7), or perhaps the feast was simply moved or omitted that year. Liturgical custom has known such things.

The Lord, as though in response to all this celebration, again appeared to Solomon by night, to confirm and qualify His earlier promises to David (vv. 11–22; 1 Kings 9:1–9). In those verses that are proper to the Chronicler (vv. 12b–15), the temple is called "a house of sacrifice," an expression suggesting two things.

First, the prayers associated with the temple, to which so much of the previous chapter was devoted, were not to be disassociated from the sacrificial ritual proper to the temple. In fact, as we earlier reflected, the times of the evening and morning sacrifices in the temple became the normal hours of daily prayer for those who worshipped elsewhere. It is a plain fact, asserted in both Testaments, that we sinful men do not draw nigh unto God apart from the shedding of blood, without which there is no remission.

Second, Jerusalem was the proper place for sacrifice. This truth was to become a principle of liturgical reform later on, during the reigns of Hezekiah and Josiah, who endeavored to close down all other places of sacrifice.

2 CHRONICLES 8

ॐ

HAVING DEVOTED SIX CHAPTERS OF THIS BOOK to what he considered the truly significant aspect of Solomon's reign—that is, the temple—the Chronicler spends the next two chapters on the more secular matters of the Solomonic era, such as foreign and domestic policy, trade, and economics.

As he divides his treatment between these two aspects of Solomon's reign, the Chronicler's preference for spiritual concerns over the material falls into a ratio of about three to one, the spiritual also being treated first. It is instructive to compare this ratio with that seen in his treatment of David. In that earlier story, as we have seen, the king's relationship to the temple was the final thing recorded of him (a sequence reasonably required by the facts), but the Chronicler's proportion of spiritual concerns (1 Chr. 13; 15—16; 22—29) to material (1 Chr. 11—12; 14; 17—21) is still weighted significantly on the side of the former.

Inasmuch as the previous six chapters have been devoted to the theme of construction, it seems appropriate that the Chronicler begins his description of the "secular" side of Solomon's reign by speaking of his other building projects in the Holy Land (vv. 1–6), a subject that leads naturally to local geography and thence to an account of the pagans who still live in the area (vv. 7–8).

This subject is tied to Solomon's domestic policy (vv. 9–10), which reminds the author to mention Solomon's wife and the palace he built for her. Though this latter building is mentioned in 1 Kings, only the Chronicler explains the project as an effort to keep this Egyptian woman and her Egyptian retinue from defiling the buildings used by Israelites (v. 11).

After eleven verses of such profane and secular concerns, the Chronicler, as though weary of the subject, reverts once again, albeit briefly, to a further account of Solomon's liturgical interests (vv. 11–16, verses peculiar to this author).

The chapter closes with the king's opening of a southern trade route that will join Hiram's great mercantile enterprises to opportunities along

the coasts of Arabia and Africa (vv. 17–18). This singular accomplishment, which secular history regards as one of Solomon's most significant achievements, serves to introduce the queen of Sheba in the next
chapter.

2 CHRONICLES 9

A QUICK GLANCE AT A MAP WILL EXPLAIN the geopolitical importance of Sheba, that ancient realm that sat on the corner of Arabia formed by the Red Sea and the Gulf of Aden, guarding the Straits of Bab el Mandeb, which joined those two large bodies of water. Thus, all traffic coming south from either the Gulf of Suez or the Gulf of Aqaba (on the north shore of which sat Solomon's ports of Elath and Ezion Geber; 8:17) was effectively controlled by Sheba. Through the Gulf of Aden, moreover, Sheba had access to other great bodies of water, such as the Arabian Sea, the Indian Ocean, even the Bay of Bengal and beyond. To the immediate west lay the Horn of Africa.

Solomon's new enterprise in the Gulf of Aqaba served as the link between the great mercantile power of Sheba to the south and, to the north, Phoenicia, where Hiram wielded economic control over the Mediterranean, Aegean, and Black Seas. It seems unlikely, therefore, that the sudden appearance of the queen of Sheba in the court of Solomon was entirely unrelated to Solomon's new geopolitical importance.

The Bible scarcely mentions this consideration, however. What rendered Solomon famous enough to attract a visit from the queen of Sheba was his reputation for wisdom (v. 5). Even on its face, this explanation seems reasonable. Sheba's mercantile dealings with Jerusalem could be handled adequately through the normal diplomatic channels that tied the world together. A more serious motive must be sought to explain why such a grand person as the queen of Sheba would visit the king of a much less significant nation. Solomon's reputation for wisdom provides that motive.

Nor was Her Majesty disappointed in what she found at Jerusalem (vv. 6–8). Although the temple was Solomon's most singular accomplishment in the capital, there is no hint in the sacred text that the queen of Sheba enjoyed access to it. Indeed, the Chronicler's earlier comment about Pharaoh's daughter (8:11) suggests that she did not.

The description of all the rich gifts exchanged by Solomon and the queen, along with a brief reference to an exchange of gifts with Hiram, brings up the subject of Jerusalem's newfound wealth (vv. 13–28). The secular historian will explain this wealth as the fruit of Solomon's great business acumen, which certainly it was. Humanly speaking, Solomon could not have constructed his new temple without the vast resources available to him through those enterprises.

The Chronicler, however, correctly perceives a deeper significance in Solomon's wealth. As he will later do in the cases of Hezekiah and Josiah, the Chronicler only speaks of this wealth *after* telling of the priority of the spiritual over the material in Solomon's program. Solomon becomes an embodiment of the many other good things that are added to those who first seek the kingdom of heaven.

Second Chronicles, having left out the many criticisms implied against Solomon in 1 Kings, comes to this wise man's death in 922 (vv. 29–31).

2 CHRONICLES 10

ॐ

This chapter is one of several places where the Chronicler clearly presumes his readers' familiarity with certain historical facts that he leaves unsaid. Here he omits, for instance, the detailed introduction to Jeroboam found in 1 Kings 11:23–40. If the Chronicler thinks it unimportant to relate those details, it is partly because he can rest assured that his readers already know them. That is to say, he can safely tell this story of the schism of 922 in his own way, because he can safely presume that the bare facts of the case are already well known.

With respect to Rehoboam (922–913), the son and successor of Solomon (with whom he shared co-regency from 931), there is not much good to be said. He was almost the perfect example of what the Bible means by the word "fool." Because he was the son of Solomon, Israel's wisest king, furthermore, this foolishness was a matter of irony as well as tragedy.

After Solomon's death, this heir to Israel's throne traveled to Shechem to receive the nation's endorsement as its new ruler (v. 1). The move was especially necessary with respect to Israel's northern tribes, where people were touchy about their traditional rights and needed to be handled gently. Even David, we recall, had to be made king twice, first over Judah about the year 1000 (2 Sam. 2:4, 10) and then over the north some years later (2 Sam. 5:4–5).

Those northern tribes, for their part, seemed willing to be ruled by Rehoboam, but they craved assurance that the new king would respect their ancient traditions and customs (v. 4). This is the first time the Chronicler even hints at popular unhappiness with the reign and policies of Solomon. The plaintiffs sought from his son, therefore, a simple pledge that their grievances would be taken seriously in the future. A great deal depended on Rehoboam's answer.

The new king apparently took the matter seriously, because he sought counsel on what to say. He began by consulting the seniors of the royal court, the very men who had for forty years provided guidance for his father (v. 6). These were the elder statesmen of the realm, those qualified to give the most prudent political counsel.

Significantly, these older men urged Rehoboam in the direction of caution and moderation with respect to the northern tribes: "If you are kind to these people, and please them, and speak good words to them, they will be your servants forever" (v. 7).

Rehoboam, nonetheless, eschewing the instruction of his elders, followed the impulses of his younger companions, who encouraged him to stand tough and not let himself be pushed around (v. 8). Indeed, they urged Rehoboam to be insulting and provocative to the petitioners (vv. 9–11). Pursuing this foolish counsel, then, Rehoboam immediately lost the larger part of his kingdom (vv. 12–19).

As I suggested above, there is great irony here, for it may be said that one of the major practical purposes of the Book of Proverbs, traditionally ascribed to Solomon, was to prevent and preclude exactly the mistake committed by Solomon's son. According to Proverbs, the fool is the man who ignores the counsel of the old and follows the impulses of untried youth.

Many a life has been ruined—and in this case a kingdom lost—because someone preferred the pooled stupidity of his contemporaries to the accumulated wisdom of his elders. Those whose counsel Rehoboam spurned, after all, were not just any old men. They were the very ancients who had provided sound guidance to the man whom the Chronicler regarded as Israel's most sagacious monarch.

2 CHRONICLES 11

BECAUSE THE STORIES ABOUT THE NORTHERN PROPHETS in the Books of Kings are so colorful and memorable (Micaiah, Elijah, Elisha), one may too easily suppose that the ministry of the prophets, at least until the eighth century, was concentrated in the north. The present chapter of Chronicles, however, which narrates the prophetic intervention of Shemaiah (vv. 2–4, paralleled in 1 Kings 12:21–24), is a first argument against that supposition. Second Chronicles goes on to tell of other active prophets in the south prior to the eighth century, accounts not found in the Books of Kings. This list includes stories of Azariah ben Obed (15:1–7), Hanani (16:7–9), Jehu ben Hanani (19:2–3), Zechariah ben Jehoiada (24:20–22), and the anonymous prophet sent to King Amaziah (25:7–9). According to the Chronicler (21:12–15), even Elijah the Tishbite intervened in the south by way of a letter (21:12–15).

Given all these accounts of southern prophets narrated only in Chronicles, it is curious and ironic that the story of Shemaiah in this chapter is the only part of the chapter that *is* found in Kings. It is followed by three sections that are *not* found in Kings.

First, there is a list of the cities fortified by Rehoboam on his southern flank against attack from Egypt (vv. 5–12). This system of defense, well known to archeology, is sometimes called antiquity's Maginot Line.

Second, the Chronicler tells of northern Levitical families that remained loyal to the government and temple in Jerusalem (vv. 13–17). Because of Jeroboam's persecution of them, these families fled south for asylum, and the schismatic king of the north appointed non-Levites in their place (1 Kings 12:31–32; 13:33).

Third, there is a detailed account of Rehoboam's apostasy in the south (vv. 18–23). This defection of Solomon's son had to be particularly distressing to the northern Levites who had fled to the south in fidelity to the Davidic covenant and the orthodox worship in the Jerusalem temple. Their disappointment is perhaps more readily understood if we think of certain contemporary Christians conscientiously driven from one church to another, only to find the second church just about as unfaithful as the first. In the case of these Levites, moreover, the move involved uprooting their families from lands they had cultivated for more than two centuries.

2 CHRONICLES 12

ℜ

REHOBOAM'S REIGN KNEW ITS UPS AND DOWNS, the downs emphatically dominant. Five years after the new king inherited the throne of David, Pharaoh Shishak, founder of Egypt's twenty-second dynasty, invaded the Holy Land and took pretty much whatever attracted his eye: "And it happened in the fifth year of King Rehoboam that Shishak king of Egypt came up against Jerusalem, because they had transgressed against the LORD. . . . So Shishak king of Egypt came up against Jerusalem, and took away the treasures of the house of the LORD and the treasures of the king's house; he took everything" (vv. 2, 9).

Alone to do so, the Chronicler once again introduces the prophet Shemaiah (cf. 11:2–4), who points out to Rehoboam the theological reason for the catastrophe that befell the kingdom (v. 5). In this instance the prophetic message brought some measure of repentance among Jerusalem's leadership, a repentance that caused the situation to become no worse (vv. 6–8).

The sacred text goes on to remark about Shishak's invasion, "He also carried away the gold shields which Solomon had made. Then King Rehoboam made bronze shields in their place, and committed *them* to the hands of the captains of the guard" (vv. 9–10). By setting bronze shields in the temple to replace the golden shields of Solomon, Rehoboam enacted a truly wretched symbolism. Some of the ancients (Daniel, Hesiod, Ovid) spoke of an historical decline from a golden age to a silver age, and thence to a bronze age. No one disputes, of course, that Solomon's was a golden age (9:13–17). However, the reign of Rehoboam, his heir, was not just a declension to silver, but all the way to bronze. The lunge, when it came, came at once, in a single generation.

We will find this pattern of sudden fall repeatedly throughout Chronicles, a Jehoshaphat followed by a Jehoram, a Hezekiah by a Manasseh, a Josiah by a villainous series of village idiots, all the way to Jerusalem's downfall in 587.

As for Rehoboam, he remained, Josephus tells us, "a proud and foolish man" (*Antiq.* 8.10.4). He never recovered from the singular folly of his first political decision. After Shishak's invasion, this thin, pathetic shadow of his father and grandfather reigned under a humiliating Egyptian suzerainty for a dozen more years. Like every fool, he had a heart problem. The final word about Rehoboam asserts, "he did evil, because he did not prepare his heart to seek the LORD" (v. 14).

2 CHRONICLES 13

REHOBOAM'S SON ABIJAH (913–911) succeeded to the throne of David. Although his reign was short, he receives an entire chapter here in Chronicles, which has no correspondence in 1 Kings. It is the battle between Abijah and Jeroboam. This material readily breaks into two parts.

The first part (vv. 1–12) is dominated by Abijah's religious speech at the very doorstep of the battle. Although it was St. Augustine's view of the schism between Israel and Judah that "the division made was not religious but political" (*The City of God* 17.21), it is clear that the Chronicler did not share that view. Regarding the Lord's covenant with David as the basis of Israel's political order, he was unable to regard that order as anything but religious. Driven by such a conviction, the Chronicler here makes Abijah his spokesman in this speech.

Pre-battle speeches by kings and generals are normally directed to their own troops, but in the present case Jeroboam permitted his opponent to speak as long as he wanted, because meanwhile a northern party of ambuscade was moving to the rear of Abijah's forces, planning to hit them from two sides (v. 13). The longer Abijah talked, thought Jeroboam, the better position his own men would attain in the rear.

Abijah, standing on a tall borderline hill from which he could be heard by the forces of Jeroboam, lays out his own perspective of the battle about to ensue. The fault, says Abijah, lies completely with Jeroboam, who took advantage of the youth and vacillation (!) of Rehoboam in order to lead an insurrection against legitimate and even divinely covenanted authority (vv. 4–7).

Then Abijah comes to the heart of the matter—at least the concern dominant in the heart of the Chronicler: Jeroboam was a worshipper of golden calves (v. 8), a man who drove out the legitimate sons of Levi from the north and elevated non-Levites in their place (v. 9). The merit of Judah over the Northern Kingdom lay in its fidelity to the true God, worshipped as He Himself had decreed His worship (v. 10). This is the essence of the Chronicler's case against the schismatic tribes of the north.

Unlike Judah, the Northern Kingdom had abandoned the legitimate priesthood and the orthodox form of worship.

In the historical perspective of the Chronicler, this liturgical consideration absolutely trumped every other. In his mind, political power and military success said nothing of a kingdom's final worth. In the last analysis, only the correct worship of God gave significance to a nation's history. Writing long after the events described in this chapter, and long after each of the kingdoms warring here had disappeared, the Chronicler looked back and inquired just what, in those historical events, was of ultimate significance, and he answered: the orthodox worship of the Lord. This is the point of Abijah's speech.

Second comes the description of the battle that ensued (not recorded in Kings). In this battle (vv. 13–22) it is significant that the priests accompanying Abijah's army played an important role, blowing the trumpet and raising an ovation of praise to God (v. 14). This battle, though it greatly weakened the political power of Jeroboam (v. 20), did not lead to a reunion of the two kingdoms.

2 CHRONICLES 14

⋙

ABIJAH'S DEATH (V. 1) AFTER THREE YEARS (13:2) was premature and unexplained, though one supposes that fourteen wives, twenty-two sons, and sixteen daughters (13:21) may have taken their toll.

Abijah was succeeded by Asa, one of Judah's longest-reigning kings (911–870), whom both historians credit with doing "*what was* good and right in the eyes of the LORD his God" (v. 2; 1 Kings 15:11). Josephus expanded slightly on that description: "Now Asa, the king of Jerusalem, was of an excellent character, and had a regard to God, and neither did nor designed any thing but what had relation to the observation of the laws. He made a reformation of his kingdom, and cut off whatsoever was wicked therein, and purified it from every impurity" (*Antiq.* 8.12.1).

The Chronicler's brief account of Asa's religious reforms (vv. 3–5) corresponds roughly to that of 1 Kings 15:7–12, but it is immediately followed by a long section not found in Kings (14:6—15:15).

During ten years of peace (vv. 1, 6), Asa strengthened and fortified the kingdom (vv. 7–8). And none too soon, as events would prove, for about the year 900 Zerah the Cushite, as the Hebrew text calls him, invaded Judah from the south. The word "million" to describe the size of Zerah's army is a bit misleading. In biblical Hebrew, a language that doesn't even have the word "million," the actual expression is "thousand thousands," an idiomatic term meaning "lots and lots." Apparently there were Libyans also included in his force (cf. 16:8), and clearly Asa is badly outnumbered, as he indicates in his prayer (v. 11).

The biblical text gives no indication of Asa's winning strategy, perhaps because the Chronicler felt that such information might detract from the theological truth of the day—namely, "the Lord struck" the invaders (v. 12). The Chronicler, true to his understanding of biblical history, will ascribe nothing in this battle to human power. Indeed, Josephus says that the battle took place while Asa was still making his prayer for victory (*Antiq.* 8.12.2). The defeat itself was total, and the

Bible revels in a description of the enemy's flight and the taking of the spoils (vv. 13–15).

It was on his return from the battlefield to Jerusalem that the king and his army encountered a prophet with a thing or two on his mind.

2 CHRONICLES 15

ॐ

THE TRUE SIGNIFICANCE OF THE RECENT BATTLE is explained to Asa and his men by this prophet, Azariah ben Obed, who speaks under the influence of "the Spirit of God" (v. 1). Once again the prophet who speaks to the king is also the spokesman for the Chronicler to us readers. Azariah contrasts the current royal reign with the earlier period, when Israel was "without a teaching priest, and without law" (v. 3). This late victory, he goes on to say, came about in response to the righteousness the Lord had in mind to reward (v. 7).

Three points of the Chronicler's theology are made in this brief prophetic sermon: First, remember that the Lord is with Israel as long as Israel is with the Lord (v. 2). Second, never forget the lamentable era of the judges, before there were teaching priests (vv. 3–6). Third, recall God's promise of continued help if Asa continues on this correct path (v. 7). In short, Azariah's view of history is identical to that of the Chronicler.

Josephus caught the sense of this prophecy: "That the reason why they had obtained this victory from God was this, that they had showed themselves righteous and religious men, and had done every thing according to the will of God; that therefore, [Azariah] said, if they persevered therein, God would grant that they should always overcome their enemies, and live happily; but that if they left off his worship, all things shall fall out on the contrary" (*Antiq.* 8.12.2). This emphasis on the correct worship of God as the secret victory is completely in line with the thinking of the Chronicler.

Asa and his associates, fired up by this short sermon, redoubled their reforming efforts, purging away what remained of the idolatry bequeathed from the era of Rehoboam (v. 8).

Meanwhile, there were new developments in the realm, these having to do with the Northern Kingdom. We earlier learned that northern Levites had fled to the south, to escape the persecution of Jeroboam (11:13–17). Levites, the Chronicler now informs us, were not the only ones to flee southward. Indeed, "great numbers" from the north, witnessing the fidelity of Asa and his consequent prosperity, arrived in the south, seeking a life more in conformity to their inherited religious instincts and convictions (v. 9).

These gathered at Jerusalem in 896 BC to solidify their commitment to Asa's cause (vv. 10–15). This gathering of northerners and southerners around the Davidic king at the temple remained an ideal that inspired the Chronicler. We shall see it again in the reigns of Hezekiah and Josiah.

Toward the end of this chapter the Chronicler tells a story borrowed from 1 Kings 15:13–14, the account of how Asa deposed his idolatrous grandmother from her special political position as "queen mother" (v. 16).

Finally, at the end of the chapter, inserted as though he were embarrassed by the fact, the Chronicler asserts that even Asa was not entirely successful (v. 17). This remark prepares us for the next chapter, in which Asa's conduct in his old age was not quite up to the mark.

2 CHRONICLES 16

ॐ

THE LATTER PART OF ASA'S RULE DID NOT RISE to the standard set by his earlier days. He waxed lazy in his later years, and the present chapter describes his decline.

There is an historical problem with the present text. If we understand verse 1 strictly, the date appears to be 875. However, according to 1 Kings 16:6–8, Baasha had died ten years earlier! Some exegetes, in hopes of removing this problem, suggest that a copyist's error has introduced a mistake into the sacred text.

While this suggestion is possible, it is not the only solution applicable to the problem. It may be that verse 1, in referring to the thirty-sixth year of Asa, is employing a shorthand formula to mean the thirty-sixth year of Asa's kingdom, that is, the divided kingdom that followed the reign of Solomon. If this interpretation is correct, then the year of reference would be 986, which accords well with the sequence given in Kings. It also seems better to fit the Chronicler's assertion that Asa's early reign enjoyed ten years of peace (14:1).

In Asa's response to Baasha's invasion we discern already his decline. Instead of going to meet his opponent in battle, as he had earlier done in the case of Zerah, Asa decided to pay someone else to assume the task. He used money to influence international politics (vv. 2–5). Thereby conceding part of the Land of Promise to a foreign power, Asa paid the Syrians to invade the territory of Baasha. Over the next couple of centuries Asa's successors on the throne would have to deal with Syrian interference in the politics of the Holy Land.

To reprimand this sin, the Lord sent to Asa the prophetic word of Hanani (vv. 7–9), the father of yet another prophet named Jehu (1 Kings 16:17). This prophetic word, found only in the Chronicler, serves to advance the latter's sense of history—namely, the conviction that "the eyes of the LORD run to and fro throughout the whole earth, to show Himself strong on behalf of *those* whose heart is loyal to Him" (v. 9). John the seer will behold these same eyes on the face of the Lamb that opens the scroll of history: "And I looked, and behold, in the midst of the throne and of the four living creatures, and in the midst of the elders, stood a Lamb as though it had been slain, having seven horns and seven eyes, which are the seven Spirits of God sent out into all the earth" (Rev. 5:6).

Asa, in response, punishes the prophet, unlike his grandfather Rehoboam, who had humbled his mind before the prophetic word (12:6). Asa thus became the first king of Judah to raise his hand against the prophets.

In turn the Lord punished Asa three years later (v. 12). He lived five years more (v. 13). The great failure of Asa's life, according to the Chronicler, came from following his disinclination to put his trust in God (vv. 7, 12).

2 CHRONICLES 17

ॐ

NONE OF THE MATERIAL IN THIS CHAPTER is found outside of Chronicles. Most of it (vv. 1–6, 10–19) introduces the reign of Jehoshaphat (870–848, with a co-regency from 873). Our suggestion of three years of co-regency would explain why Jehoshaphat undertook these new initiatives in "the third year of his reign" (v. 1). This dating is also consonant with the assertion of Jehoshaphat's reign of twenty-five years (20:31).

Perhaps dearest to the Chronicler's heart are the few verses (7–9) that he devotes to the ministry of the teaching Levites. When the king sent these Levites out "to teach in the cities of Judah," he took care that everyone would know of their official credentials. He accomplished this by sending with them certain "leaders" (*sarim*) accredited to speak in the king's name.

On the success of this mission (which will remind Christian readers of the seventy disciples sent out by Jesus) Josephus comments: "Now, in the third year of this reign, he called together the rulers of the country, and the priests, and commanded them to go round the land, and teach all the people that were under him, city by city, the laws of Moses, and to keep them, and to be diligent in the worship of God. With this the whole multitude was so pleased, that they were not so eagerly set upon or affected with any thing so much as the observation of the laws" (*Antiq.* 8.15.2).

The greater authority of these teaching Levites, however, was not derived from the delegation of the king but from the text on which their teaching was based, "the Book of the Law of the LORD" (v. 9). Is this book to be identified with the scroll later discovered in the temple during the reign of Josiah? There are two reasons for thinking this to be the case. First, exactly the same words describe the text in both instances, *sepher Torat Adonai* (v. 9; 34:14). Second, in each case the Book of the Law of the Lord appears in the context of the ministries of the Levites (v. 8; 34:12–13).

The Chronicler will return to this teaching ministry of the Levites, with particular attention to the Law of the Lord, when he comes to the postexilic period and the mission of Ezra (cf. Neh. 8). The Chronicler's view of the Levitical ministry was clearly comprehensive. These versatile men not only functioned on behalf of the liturgical rites, the general decorum, and especially the sacred music of the temple. They were also Israel's teachers in all matters pertinent to the Law given through Moses. In this latter capacity, of course, they were obliged to be literate, so it is not surprising that scribes and accountants should come from their number (34:9–10). In general, these Levites included men who were competent "in any kind of service" (34:13). We Christian readers also bear in mind that the early Church regarded the order of deacon as a sort of equivalent to the Levitical office (cf. Clement of Rome, *Corinthians* 32.2; 40.5).

2 CHRONICLES 18

AFTER AN ENTIRE CHAPTER THAT HAD NO PARALLELS IN 1 KINGS, the Chronicler now gives us a chapter that comes almost entirely (except for vv. 1–3) from 1 Kings 22. In fact, this is the only instance where the Chronicler simply repeats a long section from the Books of Kings. The occasion prompts us to inquire why.

The obvious reason is found in the nature of the material itself, which these two authors do not look at in the same way. For the author of Kings, this was a story about Micaiah and Ahab, whereas for the Chronicler it is, rather, a story about Micaiah and Jehoshaphat. Indeed, the Chronicler is only incidentally interested in Ahab, who is not even mentioned again after his death in verse 34 (contrast with 1 Kings 22:38–40). The Chronicler's concern, then, is very different. He is interested in Jehoshaphat, not Ahab. After all, it was the King of Judah, not Ahab, who wanted to consult with Micaiah (vv. 6–7), and the Chronicler inserts the account for the simple reason that it strengthens a steady motif dear to his heart—namely, the Lord's prophetic word to the kings of Judah (cf. 12:5–6; 15:1–7; 16:7–9; 19:2–3; 20:13–17; 24:20; 25:7–9, 15–16; 28:9–11; 33:10; 34:22–28). This story is one more in a thematic series that should put to rest the widespread notion that the early prophetic movement was mainly a northern phenomenon.

The Chronicler is not interested in the prophetic activity in the Northern Kingdom, for the simple reason that he is not interested in *anything* that transpired in the Northern Kingdom for its own sake. Indeed, the only time he mentions a prophetic intervention of the greatest of the northern prophets, Elijah, it is in connection with a letter that prophet wrote to a king of Judah (21:12–15).

The Chronicler's sole interest in the present story, then, has to do with the current holder of the Davidic throne, Jehoshaphat, and this story serves the Chronicler's purpose of introducing the latter's dangerous coalition with the Northern Kingdom. If Asa's great mistake was an unwise league with Syria, Jehoshaphat's was an unwise alliance with Israel.

Because of this alliance, as we shall see during the ensuing chapters, the Davidic throne was nearly lost. The marriage of Jehoshaphat's son to Ahab's daughter would introduce into the kingdom of Judah the full force of Phoenician idolatry and evil. Over the next several chapters, the solemn prophetic promise made to David would be endangered as never before. During the next several generations there will be, at several given times, only a single direct male descendant of David still alive on the face of the earth. Jehoshaphat's son, Jehoram, will kill all his brothers (21:4). Then all but one of Jehoram's own sons will be slain (21:17). When that remaining son (22:1) is killed, there will be "no one to assume power over the kingdom" (22:9). Of Jehoram's grandsons, *all* will be murdered except the infant Joash (22:1–12). All of this danger and evil will flow from Jehoshaphat's alliance with the Northern Kingdom. Better to have warfare, thought the Chronicler, than this sort of peace!

In short, then, the present story presents one more instance when a king of Judah should have taken the prophetic warning and averted disaster. The warning will be repeated in the opening verses of the next chapter, when Jehu, Hanani's son, appears on the scene to point out what Jehoshaphat should already have seen.

2 CHRONICLES 19

꣠

THE MATERIAL IN THE PRESENT CHAPTER, which is also unique to the Chronicler, includes Jehoshaphat's meeting with the prophet Jehu (vv. 1–3) and his subsequent judicial reforms (vv. 4–11).

If Jehoshaphat failed to learn from the moral example given in the previous chapter, Jehu the prophet is determined to make the king take a closer look. He warns Jehoshaphat of the danger inherent in this recent political and military alliance with a man justly described as an enemy of God. Even though Jehoshaphat has set his heart on the Lord, the divine wrath will visit his house because of his collusion with an evil man.

The Chronicler does not record Jehoshaphat's reaction to this prophetic warning, but Josephus believed that his later reforms were inspired by it. Josephus wrote, "Whereupon the king betook himself to thanksgivings and sacrifices to God; after which he presently went over all that country which he ruled round about, and taught the people, as well the laws which God gave them by Moses, as that religious worship that was due to him" (*Antiq.* 9.1.1).

To the present writer this judgment is not so obvious. For reasons best known to himself, Jehoshaphat seems not to have broken off his alliance with the Northern Kingdom, the evil of which alliance was the very point made by the prophet. Too bad. The king had now twice been warned that he had thrown in his lot with a loser. The Chronicler was not obliged to inform his readers, including ourselves, about the fate soon to befall the house of Ahab. Those facts were already well known from the Books of Kings.

Meanwhile Jehoshaphat went about reforming the nation's judicial system (vv. 4–7). In this reform we observe what appears to be a pattern from Deuteronomy 16:18–20; 17:8–13. If, as we suggested earlier (relative to 2 Chr. 17:9), the teaching of the Levites was modeled on the same document later discovered in the temple during Josiah's time, this affinity with Deuteronomy is not surprising.

In Jerusalem itself the judicial task was partly handed over to the

Levites (v. 8), under the supervision of the "chief priest"—*kohen har'osh* (v. 11). This is one more in a growing number of tasks with which the versatile Levites are entrusted.

2 CHRONICLES 20

THE MATERIAL IN THIS CHAPTER, WHICH IS MAINLY proper to the Chronicler and with scant parallel in 1 Kings (vv. 21–24 being the exception), may for analysis be divided into five parts.

First are the introductory verses that set the stage by describing the threat made to Judah by some of the local enemies to the east of the Jordan (vv. 1–2). In verse 2 it is likely that the reference to "Syria" in both the Hebrew and Greek texts should be changed to "Edom," as the RSV does. In Hebrew the two words look much more alike than they do in English, and copyists often confused them. In the present case the mention of the city of Engedi, on the coast of the Dead Sea, makes "Edom" the more probable reading.

Second, the nation gathers to pray (vv. 3–12). In Jehoshaphat's intercession (vv. 5–12) we observe a striking likeness to Solomon's prayer at the consecration of the temple (6:12–40). Indeed, the Chronicler notes that the two prayers are made in exactly the same place (v. 5; 6:13; cf. 4:9). We should regard Jehoshaphat's prayer as an extension and application of the prayer earlier made by Solomon.

This prayer especially "reminds" the Lord that the nations now threatening His temple are the very enemies that the Lord had earlier forbidden Israel to destroy (vv. 10–11; cf. Num. 20:21; Deut. 2:1, 4, 5, 8, 19). That is to say, this prayer makes a case for being heard!

Third, by way of response to this petition of Jehoshaphat, the Lord's Spirit is poured out on the Levite Jahaziel for prophetic utterance (vv. 13–17). His message is the kind of "liturgical prophecy" of which the Book of Revelation is full. Jehoshaphat and the nation are prophetically reminded, within the place and context of communal worship, that the Lord, who remains ever the Ruler of history, will give His people victory on the morrow. They need only show up for the battle; there will be no need to fight.

Fourth comes the fulfillment of Jahaziel's prophetic message (vv. 18–30), which takes place when the Levites march in religious procession in front of the army of Judah. Their worship in song and praise takes the place of the combat, as the enemies unaccountably turn on one another. This is apparently the Lord's "ambush" of them. Once again, history is determined through worship. History is not something closed off from intervention from on high, and "on high" is not closed off from prayers offered on the earth. When God's people pray, the Lord intervenes on the earth, and new things start to happen (Rev. 8:3–6).

Fifth, there follows a summary of the importance of Jehoshaphat's reign (vv. 31–34), followed by a final mention of another alliance of this king with the Northern Kingdom. This alliance too is disastrous. This last section provides the chapter's only parallel to 1 Kings (22:42–48).

2 CHRONICLES 21

⊰᠗

THE REIGN OF JEHORAM (849–841) was what one might expect from a son-in-law of Ahab and Jezebel (vv. 1–6). Inasmuch, however, as this reign will lead to the hour of greatest danger for the house of David, the Chronicler once more explicitly reminds his readers of the divine promise that guaranteed the stability of that dynasty (v. 7).

To Judah's southeast the Edomites, subdued by Jehoshaphat in the previous chapter, rose again in rebellion, this time successfully (vv. 8–10). Things were looking bad.

The letter sent to Jehoram from the prophet Elijah (vv. 11–15) is our first example of "literary prophecy," a full century before the writings of Amos and Isaiah. As it happens, however, an historical problem connected with this message raises an intriguing question. That is—since 2 Kings (chs. 1–3) seems to imply that Elijah disappeared in his fiery chariot *before* the death of Jehoshaphat, how do we now find Elijah writing a letter to Jehoshaphat's successor?

Ah, this is the sort of problem that invites an effort of imagination (and perhaps a bit of playfulness). Did Elijah actually write the letter to Jehoshaphat much earlier, but it only arrived after Jehoshaphat's death? An interesting suggestion this, if only for what it indicates of mail delivery in the ancient Holy Land.

Or did Elijah write the letter to Jehoram ahead of time, knowing by prophecy the sort of king Jehoram would be? This suggestion, advanced by some of the ancient rabbis, has the merit of honoring Elijah's knowledge of the future.

Or is it the case that Elijah, having gone up to heaven in his fiery chariot, returned to the earth for a short period to take care of his unfinished correspondence? Now there's a thought. (I warned you about playfulness.)

And, if so, might not this same earthly solicitude on the prophet's part argue that Elijah has in mind to make other return trips in the future? In fact, we know that the prophet Malachi (Mal. 4:5) believed this to be the case, nor was he the last (Matt. 11:14; 17:11–13). Indeed, the angel Gabriel, who by the time in question had shared the heavenly company of Elijah for nearly a thousand years (speaking in earthly time), dropped a remark on this subject when speaking to our Blessed Lady (Luke 1:17).

Whatever the circumstances of Elijah's letter to Jehoram, the present writer suspects that this incident, like most things touching that famous Tishbite, is not open to normal, unimaginative analysis. When we are dealing with Elijah, *anything* may happen. All possibilities should be considered. Whatever else Elijah represents in Holy Scripture, he surely stands as a reminder that there is always room for one more surprise up the divine sleeve.

Finally, then, came the Philistines and their friends, leaving the royal progeny reduced to a single prince (vv. 16–17). In the following chapter, that prince too will perish along with all his sons except one. Judah is about to enter a very dark hour.

2 CHRONICLES 22

THIS CHAPTER RECORDS ONE OF THE BLOODIEST, most distressing stories in the Bible. Athaliah, the *gebirah* or queen mother of the slain King Ahaziah, seizes the throne of Judah in 841 BC and promptly orders the murder of her own grandchildren in order to guarantee her hold on that throne (v. 10). Holy Scripture simply narrates the event, without accounting for Athaliah's motive in this singular atrocity.

Although such savagery from a daughter of Jezebel might not be surprising, Athaliah's action was puzzling from a political perspective, nonetheless, and this in two respects. First, as the story's final outcome would prove, her dreadful deed rendered Athaliah extremely unpopular in the realm, and her possession of the crown, therefore, more precarious. Second, had she preserved the lives of her grandchildren instead of killing them, Athaliah's real power in the kingdom would likely have been enhanced in due course, not lessened. As the *gebirah*, she might have remained the *de facto* ruler of Judah unto ripe old age. Just what, then, did this cruel woman have in mind?

The question proved to be understandably fascinating to literary speculation. The historian Josephus, the first to ponder the matter, ascribed Athaliah's action to an inherited hatred of the Davidic house. It was her wish, said he, "that none of the house of David should be left alive, but that the entire family should be exterminated, that no king might arise from it later" (*Antiq.* 9.7.1). This explanation seems perfectly plausible. It would also explain why 1 Kings and 2 Chronicles, both sources devoted to the study of David's house, found the story so intriguing and pertinent to their themes.

The playwright Racine developed this motive in his *Athalie*, where the evil queen exclaims, "David I abhor, and the sons of this king, though born of my blood, are strangers to me" (2.7.729–730). Following Racine, this interpretation was taken up in Felix Mendelssohn's opera *Athaliah*, which asserts that the vicious woman acted in order that "no hand could reach out for her crown, nor king henceforth from David's line preserve again the service of Jehovah" (First Declamation).

Racine also ascribed to Athaliah a second motive, namely her sense of duty to protect the realm from the various enemies that surrounded it. Indeed, she boasts that her success in this effort was evidence of heaven's blessing on it (*op. cit.* 2.5.465–484). However, since it is unclear how the slaughter of her grandchildren contributed to the regional peace that Athaliah claimed as the fruit of her wisdom, this explanation is not so plausible as the first.

The third motive ascribed by Racine seems more reasonable and is certainly more interesting—namely, that Athaliah acted out of vengeance for the recent killing of her mother and the rest of her own family. Deranged by wrath and loathing, she imagined that the slaughter of her posterity avenged the slaughter of her predecessors: "Yes, my just wrath, of which I am proud, has avenged my parents on my offspring" (2.7.709–710).

This explanation, which I believe to be correct, makes no rational sense, however, except on the supposition that Athaliah blamed Israel's God for what befell her own family. In attacking David's house, she thought to attack David's God, whom she accuses of "implacable vengeance" (2.7.727). Since the Chronicler does not record the death of Jezebel and the rest of the family, however, this motive is a better explanation of the account in 1 Kings than of that in 2 Chronicles.

Nonetheless, the third motive of Racine's Athaliah is the goal of the first. That is to say, the hateful queen seeks to destroy David's house in order to render void God's promises given through the prophets, especially the promise of the Messiah that would come from David's line, "that King promised to the nations, that Child of David, your hope, your expectation." The queen's vengeance, which later appears in Handel's oratorio *Athaliah*, correctly indicates the Christian meaning, the *sensus plenior*, of the Old Testament story. Waging war on great David's greater Son, Athaliah foreshadowed yet another usurper of the Davidic throne, hateful King Herod, who likewise ordered a large massacre of little boys in a vain effort to retain the crown that did not belong to him.

2 CHRONICLES 23

ALTHOUGH THE STORY OF THE RESCUE OF JOASH, along with his enthronement and the downfall of Athaliah, is certainly historical, the study of
comparative literature suggests a value in matching its motif to a subject found rather widespread in ancient mythology—namely, the theme
of the rightful young prince who, having been rescued from the evil
usurper in his infancy, returns later to settle the score and be restored to
his rightful inheritance. Literary history provides us with interesting
parallels.

There was, for example, the very primitive solar myth concerning
the powers of darkness, which appeared to triumph over the sun and to
reign over the time of night, defying the promised sun. This darkness,
which usurped the reign of the sun, as it were, attempted to devour the
sun in its very birth—to kill the sun, that is to say, as it emerged from its
mother's womb. In at least two versions of this ancient myth, in fact,
the darkness is portrayed as a dragonlike snake, reminiscent of a similar
account in Revelation 12.

Thus, Egypt had its myth of the dragon Set, who pursued Isis while
she carried the sun god Horus in her womb. His plan was to devour
Horus at his birth. It is further curious that Isis, like the Woman in
Revelation 12 (v. 14), is portrayed in Egyptian art (an elaborate door in
the King Tut collection, for instance) with wings, so that she could flee
from Set. Similarly, Greek mythology described the dragon-snake Py-
thon as pursuing the goddess Leto, who was pregnant with the sun god
Apollo.

In both cases, the little child escaped and later returned to destroy
the usurping serpent. The similarities of both of these myths to the
vision of the pregnant woman and her child in Revelation 12 are striking. Both ancient myths also developed the subject of the illegitimate
usurper, a theme that Matthew uses in his story of Herod seeking to
destroy the true King, Jesus, at His very birth. As I suggested earlier in
these remarks on Chronicles, the story of Joash and Athaliah serves as a
veritable *type* for the story of Herod and Jesus in Matthew 2.

This story of the rescue of Joash, found also in 1 Kings, provided an extra reason for the Chronicler to love it—namely, it was the priest-hero that rescued the infant king. In some sense Jehoiada thus became one of the Chronicler's major champions, the son of Levi who faces extreme danger to save the son of Judah and to keep intact the throne of David.

And where does the restoration of the monarchy take place? In the temple, naturally, which David's son had built for the Lord, in order that the priestly tribe could minister to Him under the protection of David. Real history is made in the house of worship.

2 CHRONICLES 24

ॐ

JOASH WAS A MERE CHILD WHEN THE THRONE was given to him after the violent deposition of his grandmother Athaliah, and we may be sure that the government in those early years fell largely to the strong, influential figures who had been responsible for that overthrow. Chief among these was the priest Jehoiada (v. 2).

In fact, Jehoiada's major hand in the restoration of a Davidic king to the throne at Jerusalem touches a strong motif of the Chronicler himself—namely, the reliance of the Davidic monarchy of Judah on the priestly house of Levi. In the present case, moreover, it is the priest who chooses the wives for the king (v. 3).

Young Joash, raised in the temple from infancy until he was seven years old, felt a special veneration for the place, a veneration that inspired his desire to see it refurbished and kept in good repair. For this work he sought the cooperation of the Levites (vv. 4–5). After some difficulties and negotiations on the matter, a collection box was placed in the temple itself to receive the necessary resources (vv. 6–11), and the required repairs were made (vv. 12–14; Josephus, *Antiq.* 9.8.2)

After the death of Jehoiada (vv. 15–16; *Antiq.* 9.8.3), however, the moral tone of the nation declined, including the wisdom and character of the king. An invasion of Syrians (vv. 23–24; 2 Kings 12:17–21), after an initial battle in which Joash was severely wounded, constrained Judah to pay tribute.

Prior to narrating this story, however, the Chronicler concentrates on the spiritual decline that preceded that military and political defeat (vv. 17–19). Jehoiada's son, Zechariah, prophesied against the national apostasy, apparently including the king's part in it (v. 20). This Zechariah, we should recall, was of royal blood, for his mother was an aunt to King Joash (22:11). Thus he was a first cousin to the king himself, the very king who conspired in his murder (v. 21).

Furthermore, in the description of this murder we observe a striking irony: Joash had Zechariah stoned to death within the temple precincts, whereas Zechariah's own father, Jehoiada, would not permit Joash's grandmother, Athaliah, to be killed in the temple.

This Zechariah seems to be the one referenced in Luke 11:51, called "the son of Berechiah" in Matthew 23:35, perhaps under the influence of Isaiah 8:2.

King Joash, wounded in the battle with the Syrians, was then slain by two of his own citizens, themselves angered over the murder of Zechariah (vv. 25–26). Again, there is a notable irony in the story: King Joash was *not* buried among the kings of Judah, whereas the priest Jehoiada *was* buried among the kings. Josephus (9.8.3) explains that this latter honor was conferred on him because of Jehoiada's restoration of the Davidic throne.

The Chronicler ends the chapter by referring to special sources he has used. This reference explains why his account differs in several particulars from the corresponding story in 2 Kings 12.

2 CHRONICLES 25

AFTER THE EARLY, ABRUPT, AND VIOLENT END to the life of Joash, we now come to the reign of his son, Amaziah (794–767). The Chronicler repeats the affirmation of 2 Kings 14:3 that this king "did what was right in the sight of the Lord," but he also includes some deeds of Amaziah that 2 Kings does not mention. The sole qualification the Chronicler makes at the beginning of the chapter is that Amaziah's heart was not pure, a point he goes on to illustrate with examples.

Both 2 Kings (14:5–6) and the Chronicler (vv. 3–4) speak of Amaziah's conformity to Deuteronomy 24:16 by not visiting revenge on the families of his father's murderers. This judicial policy, in which each person is held responsible only for his own offenses and not for those of his parents—a policy already enshrined in the Mosaic Law—will in due course inspire the prophets to deeper reflection on the nature of conscience (cf. Jer. 31:30; Ezek. 18:20).

The Chronicler elaborates at some length Amaziah's invasion of Edom, a story that takes only one verse in 2 Kings (14:7). Only the Chronicler tells of Amaziah's hiring of mercenaries and the prophetic reprimand he receives for this (vv. 6–12).

It is worth noting that Amaziah's obedience to the prophet on that occasion actually made things worse, because the dismissed mercenaries, in anger and vengeance, ravaged some of the towns of Judah (v. 13). It is possible that this misfortune is what prompted Amaziah to become less willing to listen to prophecy. We shall now consider an example of this.

After defeating the Edomites, Amaziah takes their gods for his own (v. 14), thus introducing another narrative that is missing in 2 Kings 14.

There was no obvious logic to this devout assumption of Edomite gods. After all, since these gods had been no help to the Edomites themselves, it should have occurred to Amaziah that they would not be much help to him either. A prophet is sent to point out this obvious fact to the king (v. 15).

Amaziah, however, thinks he has already listened to more than enough prophecy for one day, so he rudely dismisses the prophet (v. 16). This dismissal may indicate what the Chronicler had in mind when he said that Amaziah did not have a "loyal heart" (v. 2). In any case, the prophet warns him solemnly that worse things lie ahead.

Although we readers take as obvious the prophet's point that a victor does not reasonably adopt defeated gods, in fact those who profess to serve God often fall into this folly. They catch hold of every discredited idea and unsuccessful practice and press it to their bosoms. Even when the discrediting of these ideas and the failure of these practices yet abide in the memories of living men, they are seized upon with fervor and hope. It is irrational, and those who do such things should take seriously the words of the prophet sent to Amaziah.

If we compare the Bible's two accounts of Amaziah's challenge to the king of Israel (vv. 17–24; 2 Kings 14:8–14), we observe that the Chronicler's version of the story bears particular features of interpretation.

First, he introduces the story differently by mentioning that Amaziah "asked advice" (*yiwa'ats*) before making his challenge to Joash of Israel (v. 17). This verb, *ya'ats*, is a cognate of the noun *'etsah*, which was the last word in the preceding sentence (v. 16). Thus, the "advice" Amaziah now seeks, apparently from within his court, is contrasted with the "advice" he has just refused to accept from the prophet who was sent to warn him. That is to say, Amaziah receives both bad and good counsel, but he walks "in the counsel of the ungodly" (*ba'atsath resha'im*—Ps. 1:1). Accordingly, he meets the biblical definition of a fool. Only the Chronicler mentions either of these counsels given to Amaziah, just as only the Chronicler speaks of prophets being sent to him (cf. vv. 7–10).

Second, only the Chronicler explicitly tells of the Lord's intervention in bringing low the throne of Amaziah. This intention was also related directly to the king's refusal to hear prophetic counsel (v. 20). This interpretation of the events is related directly to the prophecy that followed that matter of the gods of Edom (v. 16).

Amaziah, released from arrest after his disastrous war with Joash of Israel, reigned fifteen more years (782–767), but like his father he was assassinated in a conspiracy.

The Chronicler omits the only positive accomplishment of Amaziah's reign, his restoration of Judah's control over the important southern port of Elath (2 Kings 14:22), a restoration made possible by his defeat of the Edomites.

In 2 Chronicles, then, Amaziah embodies the worst and most characteristic sin of Israel, the senseless adoption of gods already defeated and discredited. After his conquest of Edom, he embraced the Edomite divinities, not pausing to inquire whether gods that had already proved themselves useless to the Edomites were likely to be of any use to him!

Not only did Amaziah fail to ask that question, but he also refused to listen to the counsel of someone sent to ask it for him. Such is the spiritual deafness associated with idolatry. The hardening of the heart (v. 2) leads to the hardening of the ears.

2 CHRONICLES 26

WE COME NOW TO THE ERA OF UZZIAH. According to the custom of count-
ing both the first and last years of his time on the throne (793–742),
Uzziah had the longest reign of any monarch of Judah, fifty-two years
(v. 3). During his final years, however, he shared the throne with his
son, Jotham (v. 21). In spite of this lengthy reign, Uzziah is treated in
2 Kings (15:1–7) in a mere seven verses.

The Chronicler, whose more detailed account gives a better idea of
Uzziah's importance, distinguishes this king in five respects.

First, he mentions the tutelage provided for Uzziah by the priest
Zechariah (v. 5), whom he sees as a parallel to the ancient Jehoiada, the
spiritual father of King Joash (24:2).

Second, only the Chronicler spells out all the details of Uzziah's
military interests and exploits (vv. 6–9, 11–15). Archeology has uncov-
ered several of the military installations mentioned in these verses.

Third, only the Chronicler speaks of Uzziah's pronounced enthusiasm for agriculture and animal husbandry (v. 10).

Fourth, only the Chronicler gives the reason for Uzziah's leprosy
(2 Kings 15:5), regarding it as a punishment for his proud usurpation
of the priestly ministry (vv. 16–21). In this respect Uzziah's rejection by
God corresponds to the earlier rejection of King Saul (1 Sam. 13:8–
14). The Chronicler's inclusion of this detail expresses his sustained interest in the ministry and privileges of the authentic priesthood.

Fifth, only the Chronicler relates King Uzziah to the rise of literary
prophecy: "Now the rest of the acts of Uzziah, from first to last, the
prophet Isaiah the son of Amoz wrote" (v. 22). Because Isaiah himself,
in the sixth chapter of his book, describes a mystical vision in the temple
"in the year that King Uzziah died," it is possible that this verse in
Chronicles refers to the first five chapters of Isaiah (Is. 1:1). Both Amos
and Hosea also prophesied during the time of Uzziah, albeit in the
Northern Kingdom (Amos 1:1; Hosea 1:1).

The Bible's final word on Uzziah is not encouraging, for he is
accused of pride and anger (vv. 16–19). The prophet Isaiah, who

probably was not even born when Uzziah came to the throne, seems to intend a contrast between Judah's longest-reigning king and the Lord, Judah's true king: "In the year that King Uzziah died, I saw *the Lord* sitting on a throne, high and lifted up" (emphasis added).

2 CHRONICLES 27

⅔

IN 2 KINGS (15:32–38) SCANT ATTENTION IS PAID to the reign of Jotham. We know that he was coregent with his father, Uzziah, from roughly 750 to Uzziah's death in 742; he then reigned on his own from 742 to 735. The sixteen years of his reign (v. 1; 2 Kings 15:33) include both of these periods. This chronological complexity would explain why Josephus (*Antiq.* 9.11.2; 9.12.1) leaves out all time references for Jotham.

Both biblical historians attest of Jotham that "he did *what was* right in the sight of the LORD"; each also confesses the king's inability to exercise much influence over an unfaithful nation. We gain some sense of this national infidelity from the Books of Isaiah and Micah.

While 2 Kings mentions Jotham's construction of the "Upper Gate of the house of the LORD," the Chronicler goes into much more extensive detail about Jotham's building projects and his conquest of the Ammonites (vv. 4–6).

Jotham is at least praised for not pursuing his father's example of usurping rights over the temple (v. 2). Also unlike his father, Jotham "prepared his ways before the LORD his God" (v. 6). This is an expression we do not often find with respect to the biblical kings.

It is possible that the writers of both Kings and Chronicles were puzzled by the reign of Jotham, particularly his inability to get the citizens of Judah to follow his lead. He is faulted in neither source, though they do not tell much about him. Jotham did not enjoy the longevity and success that the Book of Proverbs promises to a wise and virtuous man.

Jotham thus becomes a sort of tragic figure, even though the Bible does not stop to reflect on the nature and dynamics of the tragedy, as it does in the case of Job and Qoheleth. Jotham is treated, rather, the way Abner is treated—as a just man who did not, in fact, receive all that a just man can be expected to receive. In these two historical books, 2 Kings and 2 Chronicles, the Bible does not pause to reflect on this, any more than it does in the case of Abner or, even earlier, righteous Abel.

This chapter on Jotham is, in fact, the shortest chapter written by the Chronicler, and he limits himself to his precise task—to chronicle, to record the story. He advances no thesis with respect to it. He does not suggest, in even the faintest way, how we should view the problem of theodicy implicitly posed by the story. He not only does not answer the question contained in this story; he does not even mention that the story suggests a question. On all this he remains silent.

We readers, however, taking into consideration the whole of the inspired literature, do acknowledge the question posed by the story of Jotham. We ourselves expect God to treat righteous Jotham as a righteous man should be treated. Jotham's reign, then, becomes a sort of foreshadowing of the Cross, where the world's supremely righteous Man is not treated as we believe a righteous man should be.

2 CHRONICLES 28

࿇

HAVING REMARKED THAT THE CHRONICLER'S STORY of a good king is his shortest chapter, we now come to a very bad king, Ahaz (735–715). He is so bad that he is likened to the apostate kings of the north (v. 2).

The first fifteen verses of the present chapter contain two accounts that it is profitable to contrast. The first is cruel, but the second is kind.

The first event is Ahaz's sacrificing of his son. Even though the Chronicler says "sons" (v. 3), it is possible that this is a rhetorical flourish. Both 2 Kings 16:3 and Josephus (*Antiq.* 9.12.1) speak of just one son being sacrificed. The time of this crime appears to have been the invasion of the Syro-Ephraimitic League (vv. 4–5), early in the reign of Ahaz, when the new king, desperate in the face of this invasion (Is. 7:1–2), performed this filial sacrifice in order to win the favor of the Canaanite divinities to which he was devoted (v. 2). We have to do, in this instance, not only with the abomination of child sacrifice, but also with the king's endangerment of the royal line. It was on this occasion that the prophet Isaiah went to meet King Ahaz to reassure him of the downfall of Syria and Ephraim (Is. 7:3–9). Immediately afterwards Isaiah prophesied God's miraculous intervention on behalf of His promises to the royal family: "Behold, the virgin shall conceive and bear a Son, and shall call His name Immanuel" (7:10–17, especially 14).

The second event is the kindness shown by the northern citizens toward the prisoners of war from Judah who had been brought to them by Israel's invading army. Only recently a southern prophet named Amos had been preaching in the Northern Kingdom, and during the course of one of his sermons he had especially mentioned the ill treatment suffered by captives and hostages taken during war. He had criticized the Philistines and the Phoenicians for selling such captives into slavery to the Edomites (Amos 1:6, 9).

Moreover, another prophet named Obed suddenly appeared on the scene and upbraided Israel's army for taking such captives on their recent invasion of Judah (vv. 9–11). This reprimand became part of a general humane uprising against the retaining of these captives

(vv. 12–13), and this uprising brought results. All of the captives, after being well treated by the populace, were taken back to the border city of Jericho and released to go home (vv. 14–15). This very edifying story, found only in Chronicles, demonstrates the endurance of kindness and compassion even in that brutal period of the eighth century before Christ.

This story of good people in the north also prepares for Hezekiah's overtures to the north in the following chapter.

Ahaz, for his part, had a tumultuous reign (vv. 17–18) because of his infidelity to God (v. 19). Instead of turning to the Lord in repentance, he sought a political solution for what was certainly a spiritual problem; he appealed to the Assyrians for help against his enemies (v. 16).

Although the Assyrian emperor, Tiglath–Pileser III (745–727), provided some relief to Ahaz by defeating his oppressors (2 Kings 15:29; 16:9), the Chronicler believed that this military intervention accomplished more harm than good for Judah (vv. 20–21), because it placed Ahaz under the obligation of tribute to a foreign power and involved his throne with new forms of idolatry.

It is a fact, moreover, that the name of Ahaz appears in an Assyrian inscription (where he is called "Ia-u-ha-zi") which records the kings of Syria, Phoenicia, and Palestine from whom the Assyrians received tribute. That is to say, Ahaz is regarded in this inscription (in Pritchard, *Ancient Near Eastern Texts*, page 282) simply as another defeated king beholden to Tiglath–Pileser. Obviously the perception of the thing in Assyria differed from its perception in the eyes of Ahaz!

In addition, Ahaz began to worship the gods of Damascus, because these had proved victorious against him (vv. 22–23). The king somehow failed to consider that these same gods had been shown to be of no avail against the invading Assyrians. Worshippers of false gods tend not to give sufficient heed to concrete points of evidence.

We know from the longer account of this matter in 2 Kings 16:10–16 that the priest Uriah seconded Ahaz's fall into idolatry. The Chronicler, for his part, will not honor the memory of this priest by so much as mentioning his name.

At the end of a relatively short reign, Ahaz "rested with his fathers" (2 Kings 16:20). We should bear in mind that this expression was only a contemporary euphemism for "he died." As a matter of fact, Ahaz did not "rest with his fathers" in the sense that he was buried with them, for the Chronicler tells us (contrary to 2 Kings) that this awful king did not merit interment in the royal cemetery (v. 27). This fact indicates that the contemporaries of Ahaz recognized his infidelities and acted accordingly.

For the prophet Isaiah, the reign of unbelieving Ahaz was a weariness to both God and men: "Hear now, O house of David! *Is it* a small thing for you to weary men, but will you weary my God also?" (Is. 7:13).

2 CHRONICLES 29

ॐ

WE COME NOW TO THE REIGN OF KING HEZEKIAH (716–687), a period to which the Chronicler, regarding Hezekiah as one of Judah's greatest monarchs, will devote four whole chapters. In particular, the Chronicler's treatment of Hezekiah lays the groundwork for the understanding of the later efforts of King Josiah and the deuteronomic reformers.

This latter point is significant, because the reign of Hezekiah can hardly be understood except in the context of the social prophetic movement of the eighth century, chiefly the influence of Isaiah and Micah. What Jeremiah would later be to the period of Josiah, Isaiah was to the time of Hezekiah. This king, then, provides a link between two periods of biblical prophecy.

Hezekiah, because of the relatively short life of his father, was only twenty-five when he assumed the throne in 716 (v. 1; 2 Kings 18:2). Some historians speculate that he was as young as fifteen. Perhaps his youth and inexperience are what disposed Hezekiah to rely on the counsel and influence of the priests and Levites older than himself, a trait of which the Chronicler, needless to say, heartily approved (vv. 4–5). There is an irony, nonetheless, in the young king's addressing these men as "my sons" (v. 11).

Hezekiah began his rule by purging the temple of pagan "rubbish" (v. 5) with a view to restoring the authentic temple liturgy, so woefully neglected during the reign of his father Ahaz (vv. 6–9, 19; 28:24).

The priests and Levites, in response to the royal summons, began to purge the temple of everything that defiled it, evidently the instruments and apparatus of pagan worship (vv. 12–16). This process required two weeks for completion (v. 17).

Unlike his faithless father, Hezekiah was aware of the spiritual origin of Judah's political problems. Hard times had befallen the people, he was convinced, because Judah, and especially Judah's king, had strayed from the path of righteousness (v. 8). We recall that King Ahaz had sought to deal with the national crisis by playing geopolitical games, seeking help from Assyria to deal with enemies closer to hand. This approach had simply gained him a larger and more serious enemy. Indeed, the most significant crisis in Hezekiah's reign, the Assyrian invasion near the end of the eighth century, was the direct result of the efforts of King Ahaz to alter the power politics of the region.

Hezekiah, for his part, would have none of this. He was determined to deal with spiritual problems *as* spiritual problems, and not something else. Indeed, Hezekiah's programmatic reform maintained the proper priority indicated by our Lord's mandate that we "seek *first* the kingdom of heaven." Nothing else in Judah's national life, Hezekiah believed, would be correctly ordered if anything but the kingdom of God were put in first place. What was first must be placed first, not second or somewhere else down the line.

The kingdom of God is *first*, not only as a point of sequence, but also as a matter of principle. It is first, not only in the sense that it precedes everything else, but also in the sense that it lays the foundation for everything else. The foundations of houses are laid prior to the rest of the house, because the rest of the house is impossible without that foundation. It is that foundation that supports the rest of the house. This is what is meant by the priority of a principle. This priority is more than mere sequence. It has to do with essence. It is silly to think that we can first build the house and then add the foundation. It is similarly silly to think that we can first have a well-ordered life and then start on the foundation of that life. The kingdom of God, accordingly, must be put first, and the Lord warns us about those who build on any other foundation.

The temple was not a building simply consecrated to God; it was consecrated to the *worship* of God. Consequently, after the temple was purged of defilements, King Hezekiah saw to it that this sacred space was restored to the people's sacrificial worship.

In fact, however, the first sacrifices offered in the restored temple were part of the restoration itself, for they were expiatory sacrifices, "sin offerings" to atone for Judah's recent infidelities (vv. 21–24).

And not for Judah only. It is important and worthy of note that the expiatory sacrifices were offered on behalf of "*all* Israel." As we shall see in the ensuing chapters, Hezekiah had in mind to restore *all* Israel to unity under the Davidic covenantal monarchy and around the one temple in Jerusalem.

We recall that the Assyrians had just destroyed the Northern Kingdom in 722, only six years before Hezekiah assumed the throne of Judah. The Assyrians, under Emperor Sargon II, had deported great masses of Israel's population to regions far east in the Fertile Crescent. At the time of that deportation, however, a significant remnant of Israelites had been left behind, and Hezekiah regarded this situation as the opportunity to undertake the aforesaid restoration of *all* Israel. His purpose, we may say, was ecumenical, in the sense of wanting to restore the earlier unity. The following chapters will describe how he went about this endeavor, but here in these initial sacrifices we see already the nature of his intention.

After these expiatory sacrifices, performed early in the morning (v. 20), came the first prescribed daily "burnt offering" of Israel's common worship (v. 27), followed by other sacrifices, including "thank offerings" made spontaneously for various petitions and for the rendering of thanks to God (vv. 31–33).

In the Chronicler's description of this worship we may particularly note the emphasis on sacred music (vv. 25, 26, 28, 30), because this aspect of the worship has represented a special point of interest for the Chronicler from the beginning.

The Chronicler's emphasis here is congruous with what we know from the rest of Holy Scripture: namely, that sacred hymnody has always been regarded as a normal and expected component of the Lord's true worship. The command to "sing to the Lord" is really a command, not a recommendation. Furthermore, our attention is drawn to the use of the Psalter, "the words of David" (v. 30), in the official worship of God's people.

2 CHRONICLES 30

BECAUSE OF THE SPECIAL CIRCUMSTANCES indicated in the sacred text (v. 3), King Hezekiah and his advisors determined to observe the Passover that year one month late (v. 2). This delay could be justified by an extension of a rule given in the Book of Numbers (9:6–12), according to which those who happened to be unclean at the time of Passover could observe it a month later.

This postponement also gave Hezekiah the opportunity to invite the Israelites who formed the remnant of the Northern Kingdom, which had been destroyed by the Assyrians just six or seven years earlier. Because of this gracious overture to the "separated brethren," those Israelites from whom Judah had been estranged for two whole centuries, there has arisen in modern times the custom of referring to Hezekiah as something of an "ecumenist." Given the context of its cause, that description appears just.

Hezekiah's ecumenical effort was only partly successful, but it is instructive to observe the historical significance of that success. His overture to the north was rejected by the major northern tribe, Ephraim (v. 10), but not by everybody. "Nevertheless," the Bible says, "some from Asher, Manasseh, and Zebulun humbled themselves and came to Jerusalem" (v. 11). That is to say, for the first time in two hundred years, pilgrims came to Jerusalem from Galilee.

It was Hezekiah, therefore, who was responsible for the spiritual and theological reunion of Galilee with Judah, after so prolonged a separation. These Galileans had just experienced the real meaning of schism. They still had in their mouths the bitter taste of separation from their own roots. Given a month's notice, they hastened to Jerusalem for the Passover, where Hezekiah and the men of Judah welcomed them to reunion. Hezekiah thus provides the ecumenical example to be followed.

In his endeavor to reunite "all Israel," Hezekiah appears in Chronicles as a kind of new David, for this is exactly what David is credited with doing (1 Chr. 11:1, 4; 15:28). First Chronicles 11—12 contains a list of the warriors who joined David from all of Israel's tribes. It is this reunion of the tribes under the Davidic covenant that Hezekiah has in mind to restore.

The importance of these Galileans to Hezekiah's reign is indicated by the fact that one of Hezekiah's later wives was from Galilee (2 Kings 23:36), as was his daughter-in-law (2 Kings 21:19).

This religious unity of Judah and the Galilean tribes was to endure over the centuries, once Galilee was again joined to the Davidic throne. From that point on, pilgrims would come, at the appointed times, to offer their devotion at Jerusalem's temple. We know some things about these Galilean pilgrims. Of one of these Galileans it was said, "His parents went to Jerusalem every year at the Feast of the Passover. And when He was twelve years old, they went up to Jerusalem according to the custom of the feast" (Luke 2:41–42). Of this same Galilean, some years later, it is recorded, "He remained in Galilee. But when His brothers had gone up, then He also went up to the feast, not openly, but as it were in secret" (John 7:9–10).

These Galilean pilgrims would be easily recognized by their curious northern accent, and people would remark on it. They would say such things as, "Surely you are *one* of them; for you are a Galilean, and your speech shows *it*" (Mark 14:70). If a group of Galileans all started speaking at once, everybody present took note of it. They remarked, "Are not all these who speak Galileans?" (Acts 2:7).

In 715, therefore, the people of Judah, their ranks swollen by the reunited brethren from the north, gathered in Jerusalem to observe the first joint celebration of the Passover in two hundred years.

A first order of business was to purge the place of the pagan altars and shrines King Ahaz had erected in deference to the Assyrian overlord (v. 14). We may remark on two points of significance about this action.

First, the destruction of the vile Assyrian symbols had to be especially gratifying to the people from the north, whose homeland had been ravaged and laid waste by Sargon II and the Assyrian army just seven years earlier (722).

This action on the part of Hezekiah was not only religious. It expressed an explicit, intentional affront to the Assyrian Empire, making it perfectly clear to everyone that he meant business and would go all out in resistance to Assyria. That is to say, Hezekiah was deliberately knocking the chip off the shoulder of Sennacherib, the new Assyrian emperor.

It was a very bold move for this young king, only twenty-five years old, directly and explicitly to defy the armed might of the massive Assyrian Empire. It clearly marked Hezekiah as a "leader," in the sense used by the writer who remarked, "a leader is someone with a seriously underdeveloped sense of fear."

On the other hand, Hezekiah's action most certainly won him new friends within the remnant of Israel's northern tribes. Many of these northern newcomers, who had lived in schism and even apostasy for over two centuries, were not ritually pure (v. 18), but they were permitted to share in the Passover anyway. Hezekiah, perceiving that this was a time when wisdom urged a certain latitude in the application of the Law, waived the rules about ritual purity, praying that the Lord would look indulgently on each man's good intention (vv. 19–20).

It is worth remarking that the Chronicler, who treated matters of ritual with singular respect and seriousness, not only did not criticize Hezekiah for this, but he also remarked, "And the LORD listened to Hezekiah and healed the people" (v. 20).

We see in Hezekiah's attitude toward the letter of the Law a kind of foreshadowing of Jesus, whom the Gospels describe as applying the Law with a gentle and merciful hand. Indeed, this disposition of Jesus gave rise to a fierce and murderous response among His enemies (cf. Mark 3:6 for instance).

These observers of Hezekiah's Passover feast were enjoying themselves so much that, when the week of the Unleavened Bread was over, they decided to prolong the fun and festivities for another week (v. 23). It would seem that, after being separated from one another for more than two centuries, these reunited Israelites simply could not get enough of one another. The likes of this great festival, over which Hezekiah presided, had not been seen since the reign of Solomon. Such is the joy that descends on the people of God when schism and animosity are brought to an end.

2 CHRONICLES 31

THE CHRONICLER GIVES US TO UNDERSTAND that those many Israelites reunited through the efforts of Hezekiah, doubtless inspired by the restoration of their common worship in the temple, went without delay to other cities in the Holy Land to initiate its spiritual reform and renewal (v. 1).

It is impossible to say whether Hezekiah was conscious, ahead of time, that his ecumenical appeal to the north would also bring important economic and geopolitical benefits to his kingdom, but it is certain that such benefits did come about as results of his appeal.

A first benefit was economic. After all, the northern sections of the Holy Land were and have always been its more prosperous parts. Thus, the arrival of these northern visitors to Jerusalem automatically brought the place enhanced revenue (vv. 5–6), being doubtless the first of many beneficial commercial contacts. The economy of the region improved.

This economic development should also be related to the teaching of the social prophets who had been so active in Judah during recent years, Micah and Isaiah. It is reasonable to think that the king, prompted by the preaching of these men, undertook the sorts of social reform that would lead to the prosperity we see here in Chronicles.

A second benefit was sociological, because the prosperity of Hezekiah's reign led to the considerable growth of Jerusalem during that period. Indeed, archeologists estimate that the size of the city doubled or even tripled while Hezekiah was king; the city's western wall was extended to include a second hill.

This growth can be explained in two ways, both of them plausible and both of them traceable to the greater economic prosperity. First, the greater prosperity brought about a higher birth rate and longer life span. Second, Jerusalem became home to many refugees fleeing from the north.

The next chapter of Chronicles will describe a third benefit, also derivative of Judah's financial prosperity—namely, a growing sense of political autonomy from the Assyrian overlord. Hezekiah could not seriously contemplate resistance to Assyria without the financial resources to make it stick. Now, from Judah's increased wealth, made available by the king's new friendship with the north, Hezekiah was able to construct fortifications and take other steps to enhance the kingdom's military strength.

For example, Hezekiah was now able to dig the underground aqueduct that would enable the capital to withstand a lengthy siege. While the city's besiegers would be obliged to endure the heat and thirst otherwise prevalent in the Judean desert, its besieged citizens would have plenty of water (32:30).

These benefits to Judah all came from its new association with the remnants of the Northern Kingdom. There is a lesson here, of course, because this story exemplifies those blessings, good and pleasant, that are poured out when the brethren, united under the Lord's anointed king, live together in harmony, commonly served by His anointed priesthood. These blessings resemble that anointing oil upon the head, running down richly to saturate the priestly beard of Aaron, flowing further yet to consecrate the very fringes of his vestment. This blessing falls as the dew of the north, even from Mount Hermon, descending on Mount Zion, for there the Lord gives His blessing, life for evermore.

We observe that King Hezekiah appointed twelve men to keep charge of the treasures collected in the temple precincts (vv. 12–13). It is worthy of note that this sacred number twelve, the measure of the months in the solar calendar but more especially the number of Israel's sons, is preserved in Hezekiah's count, even though the twelve tribes no longer existed as political and social entities. To Hezekiah's thinking, this latter circumstance was of no significance to his action. He was thinking of *kol Israel*, "all Israel," in its essence, in its *idea*, the fullness of Israel as he was endeavoring to reconstitute it after two hundred years of disunity and utter humiliation. For Hezekiah, these twelve men still represented God's people in its essence and totality.

In the Gospels, centuries after the slightest living social or political significance ceased to be attached to the number twelve, we see Jesus similarly choosing twelve men, who will sit on twelve thrones, judging the twelve tribes of Israel. Indeed, the Church's first historian records the care that the Apostles took to maintain that twelvefold symbolic leadership of the Church for the Day of Pentecost (Acts 1:21–26), the day of the Church's foundation, and in the Bible's final book the names of these twelve are inscribed on the twelve foundation stones of New Jerusalem (Rev. 21:14).

By way of further parallel with the New Testament, let us also observe that this list of twelve men here in Chronicles is followed by another list of seven men, these charged with the proper disposition of the accumulated treasure to the needs of the priestly and Levitical families (vv. 14–19). Here there is a striking correspondence with the Acts of the Apostles, where Luke's first list of twelve men (1:13–21) is followed by a list of seven men charged with the "daily distribution" to the widows (6:1–5).

Both numbers, of course, are significant. Each is a combination of the human number four with the divine number three. In twelve, the three and four are united by multiplication; in seven they are joined by addition. Twelve is the number of months in the year, seven the number of days in the week. As the combination of the divine and the human numbers, both seven and twelve have to do with the union of God and man, which is the Incarnation, grace, and eternal life. This is what we mean by calling seven and twelve the numbers of fullness and perfection.

If we attempt to distinguish between twelve and seven as these numbers appear here in Chronicles and in the parallel lists in Acts, we may say that the number twelve seems to be theoretical and abstract, while the number seven appears to be practical. In both biblical texts twelve symbolizes the fullness of the institution. As is indicated by the names of the twelve apostles on the foundation stones of the new Jerusalem, twelve is the foundational number, the number of principle. Seven, on the other hand, is the number of application; it pertains to those men actually counted for a specific task. Thus, twelve may be called the number of essence or being (*esse*), and seven the number of agency and activity (*agere*).

2 CHRONICLES 32

⸎

THE BEGINNING OF THIS CHAPTER IS ABRUPT. We have been reading about the reforms of Hezekiah, his renewal of the temple worship, and his endeavor to restore the ancient unity of "all Israel." Now, all of a sudden, we encounter somebody named Sennacherib, coming out of nowhere, invading Judah and threatening the kingdom of Hezekiah. How did all this come to pass?

Six years or so before Hezekiah came to the throne of Judah, Sargon II became the Emperor of Assyria (721–705). As so often was the case when a new emperor came to power, various disgruntled elements in the empire, sensing that the political transition was their chance for rebellion and a new political order, chose that moment to foment insurgencies. This was a common pattern, and when a new emperor had to deal with more than one insurrection at a time, he could have his hands full for several years. This is exactly what transpired when Sargon took the throne in 721.

First, there was a rebellion of the Babylonians, led by their king, Merodach-Baladan. Then, on the northwest corner of the empire, King Midas of Phrygia stirred an insurrection among the Syrians in 717. Meanwhile, a barbarous Indo-Aryan group called the Cimmerians was moving south from the Caucasus and threatening several northern sections of the Assyrian Empire. Finally, on the empire's southwestern border, the one closest to the Holy Land, the Ethiopians were effectively taking charge of Egypt and would, in 710, create Egypt's Twenty-fifth Dynasty.

With so many problems facing the new emperor, some of the smaller nations within the empire were prompted to contemplate a little rebelliousness of their own. As the Phrygians had encouraged an uprising among the Syrians, so Egypt fostered an impulse toward rebellion in the Holy Land.

The first to act on this impulse were the Philistines, who began to revolt in 714, at the very time when Hezekiah was initiating his reforms in Judah. Because Egypt promised military aid to whoever would join in that uprising, the temptation was strong for Edom, Moab, and Judah to throw in their lot with the Philistines. Both 2 Kings and Isaiah testify to the extraordinary geopolitical pressure brought to bear on the smaller kingdoms of Palestine during this period.

Isaiah himself strongly opposed this rebellion against Assyria. Not only did he distrust Egypt's intentions in the region; he perceived that Egyptian and Philistine foreign policy was something quite distinct from the will of God. He urged Hezekiah and Judah not to take part in the rebellion inspired by the political machinations of Ethiopia and Egypt (Is. 18—19).

Early in 712 Isaiah pleaded with Hezekiah not to become involved. Later that very year, when Sargon invaded the Holy Land to deal with the Philistines, Hezekiah could be glad that he had hearkened to the prophet's counsel (Is. 20). In the Assyrians' eyes, of course, Hezekiah was already compromised by his destruction of the Assyrian altars in the Holy Land, but at least he had not joined the open rebellion of the Philistines, and in 712 Judah was spared the destruction inflicted on the latter, thanks to the godly admonition of Isaiah.

Everything changed, however, in 705, when Sargon II was killed in a battle with the Cimmerians that had invaded Asia Minor. The Assyrian Empire was once again agitated by various insurrections, rendered more serious and volatile by the fact that the emperor had perished so far from the center of political power at Nineveh. The new emperor, Sennacherib (704–681), faced trouble on all sides. For example, the Babylonians immediately revolted, as they would continue to do periodically until they were strong enough to conquer Assyria itself a century later.

Hezekiah, concluding that the time had arrived for Judah's independence, joined a general revolt that was taking shape on the eastern shore of the Mediterranean, largely under the leadership of Phoenicia. Indeed, it seems that Hezekiah himself brought pressure to bear on some of the Philistine cities in order to bring them into the coalition (2 Kings 18:8). He further saw to the fortifications of Jerusalem (2 Chr. 32:3–5) and the digging of the underground aqueduct (v. 30).

Meanwhile, Hezekiah also sent delegates to Egypt, seeking assistance in the rebellion. Isaiah thoroughly denounced all these efforts (Is. 30:1–7), but the king apparently paid him no mind.

Sennacherib needed nearly three years to fight Babylon to a standstill, but by 701 he was ready to move against the rebels in the west. He went straight for the strongest among them, Phoenicia, replacing the king of Tyre, who sought refuge on Cyprus. Indeed, this crushing of the Phoenician uprising in 701 led to the serious demise of the Phoenicians as the great maritime power of the Mediterranean. In due course they would be replaced by their own colonies, such as Carthage, and also, of course, by the Greeks.

Once the Phoenicians fell, Hezekiah realized that the game was up and accordingly sued for terms of peace. Sennacherib, destroying forty-six walled cities of Judah and deporting their populations, was not interested in dragging out the campaign. He agreed to peace terms but made them severe. Hezekiah was obliged to strip the temple of its gold and empty the royal treasury. The whole adventure, taken up over the objections of Isaiah, proved to be very expensive to the kingdom.

This is the point at which 2 Chronicles once again picks up the narrative with the present chapter. According to Josephus, Sennacherib was not satisfied with the amount Hezekiah paid. He planned to lay siege to the city anyway. This chapter of Chronicles, then, treats the siege of Jerusalem as the occasion when the Lord vindicated Hezekiah's loyal service to the temple and its worship ("these deeds of faithfulness," v. 1).

As Sennacherib approached Jerusalem, Hezekiah knew the die was already cast. There could be no peace negotiations this time. Capitulation to Sennacherib would certainly mean the city's destruction. As had happened in the Northern Kingdom in 722, the masses of Judah's population would be deported. Hezekiah saw that a fight to the death was now the only option open to him. Indeed, the reader may gain the impression that Hezekiah had long looked forward to this hour of showdown with Assyria.

Among their preparations for the coming siege, Hezekiah and his men took care to deprive the invading Assyrians of all access to local water (vv. 3–4). This act of stopping up the wells, recorded only in Chronicles, would render the siege far more arduous for the besiegers, while the citizens of Judah, enclosed in the city, would enjoy ample water through the underground tunnel (six feet high) that Hezekiah had dug through solid stone, extending from the Gihon Spring to the Pool of Siloam (v. 30).

Hezekiah also fortified the city walls with battlements and further organized Jerusalem for military resistance. Afterwards he exhorted the people to put their faith in the Lord's deliverance. None of these details (vv. 2–8) are found in either 2 Kings or Josephus.

It is instructive to observe that Hezekiah does all that he can do, along with putting his trust in God's assistance. He does not neglect the human efforts to defend the city. His trust in the Lord was not a foolish, superstitious, magic-like confidence. He took every human precaution dictated by wisdom and experience. This was the context for his trust in the Lord's deliverance.

Sennacherib sent to Jerusalem a delegation charged to discourage those besieged within the city walls. Comparing this account of the activity of this delegation with the other extant versions of the story (2 Kings 18—19; Is. 36—37; *Antiq.* 10.1.1–5), the reader observes the Chronicler's lack of interest in the many details recorded in those other sources. For example, unlike 2 Kings, he does not provide the date of the invasion, nor does he provide the names of those in Sennacherib's delegation. In addition, he does not tell the great number of the Assyrians who perished (v. 21).

For the Chronicler the great offense of the Assyrians, which he elaborates through verses 16–19, consisted in their equating Israel's God with all the other gods they boast of having defeated.

Although the prophet Isaiah was arguably the major religious figure of the day, this is the only place where he is named in the Books of Chronicles (v. 20).

In the event, of course, Jerusalem did not fall to the Assyrians. There were two reasons that seem to have been complementary. First, an angel of the Lord intervened, evidently in the form of a plague that destroyed the bulk of the Assyrian forces (v. 21); and then Sennacherib received word that he was needed back at the capital (2 Kings 19:7). That first explanation is corroborated somewhat by the observation of Herodotus that a plague of mice overran the Assyrian camp. Mice are common bearers of disease and infection.

In any event, the faith and fame of King Hezekiah were extolled in the outcome (v. 23).

The one verse devoted to Hezekiah's sickness and recovery (v. 24) might be a disappointment to students of the Bible except for the many interesting details filled in by 2 Kings 20:1–11; Is. 38:1–8, 21–22; and Josephus, *Antiq.* 10.2.1. It appears to me that the Chronicler presumes the reader's prior acquaintance with the details of this story, but he passes over them in order to say more about the king's state of soul, his lack of gratitude, his pride, but then also his punishment and his humble repentance. This description of Hezekiah's spiritual trial is found only in Chronicles.

Whereas in Chronicles the description of Hezekiah's great wealth stands outside of an historical context (vv. 27–29), in 2 Kings 20:13 it is placed in the context of the visit of the Babylonian delegation. The Chronicler, in his account of this latter event, shows more interest in Hezekiah's spiritual state. The diplomatic visit itself is treated without physical details. Indeed, the Chronicler seems to suppose that his readers already know this story; he writes, completely *en passant*, "*regarding* the ambassadors of the princes of Babylon . . . God withdrew from him" (v. 31).

In short, throughout this section the Chronicler manifests more interest in Hezekiah's state of soul than in his political and military accomplishments. In this respect the king receives from the Chronicler pretty much the same sort of attention as David.

2 CHRONICLES 33

ॐ

WE COME NOW TO MANASSEH, whose reign (687–642, but with a co-regency from 697) was an unmitigated failure. First, he rebuilt, or permitted to be rebuilt, all the idolatrous shrines throughout the land, places his father Hezekiah had taken great pains to destroy (v. 3). Second, he defiled the temple itself by the erection of pagan altars within its precincts (vv. 4–5). Third, he resorted to human sacrifice in the case of his children. Fourth, he engaged in magic and sorcery (v. 6).

Not only were these same sins of Manasseh recorded in 2 Kings 21:3–6, but Jeremiah (7:31) also described some of the evils of this time: "And they have built the high places of Tophet, which *is* in the Valley of the Son of Hinnom, to burn their sons and their daughters in the fire."

It would appear that the biblical authors were most offended by Manasseh's erection of an idol in the temple (v. 7; 2 Kings 21:7). Both the Chronicler and the author of Kings cite the promise of the Lord to Solomon that His "name" would abide in His house in Jerusalem (2:1, 4).

The Bible-reader is stunned by this massive apostasy within a single generation. What can account for so thorough and swift a fall from grace? It is likely that it should be ascribed to several causes, but I suggest that among those causes should be counted a certain erroneous and unwarranted sense of security, nearly tantamount to superstition and magic. When Manasseh was but a child, Jerusalem had been miraculously delivered from Sennacherib's siege. That deliverance, which had arrived as though out of nowhere, gave rise in many minds to the persuasion that Jerusalem was invincible and would never fall to the enemy. Once saved, Jerusalem would always be saved.

My suggestion is not without basis in the actual history, because we know from the prophet Jeremiah that such a superstitious attitude toward Jerusalem, accompanied by a magical sense of the city's invulnerability, would endure throughout the rest of that century and, indeed, all the way to that day in 587 when the Babylonians destroyed it: "Do not trust in these lying words, saying, 'The temple of the LORD, the temple of the LORD, the temple of the LORD are these'" (Jer. 7:4).

There are few impressions more deceptive than that of invincibility, and this story of Manasseh is one of the Bible's clearest illustrations of the danger.

Nonetheless, Holy Scripture gives us two views of King Manasseh. In 2 Kings he was a thoroughly bad man whose reign had no redeeming aspects. He was not only an idolater of the first rank (21:3–5, 7, 11), but also a murderer and sorcerer. Manasseh offered at least one of his children in sacrifice (21:6) and "shed very much innocent blood, till he had filled Jerusalem from one end to another" (21:16). Josephus must have had this text in mind when he wrote that Manasseh "barbarously slew all the righteous men that were among the Hebrews; nor would he spare the prophets, for he every day slew some of them, till Jerusalem overflowed with blood" (*Antiq.* 10.3.1).

The most notable of the prophets murdered by Manasseh was the great Isaiah. According to an account recorded in the apocryphal story, *The Martyrdom of Isaiah*, Manasseh caused the prophet to be sawn in two. A passage in the Epistle to the Hebrews, because it mentions this detail, is often thought to refer to the era of Manasseh: "Still others had trial of mockings and scourgings, yes, and of chains and imprisonment. They were stoned, they were sawn in two, were tempted, were slain with the sword" (11:36–37).

There is a rather different—or at least a more ample—account of Manasseh's reign in 2 Chronicles. As we have seen, the Chronicler tells the same story of the evils of Manasseh, but he assigns them only to the first part of his long reign (vv. 1–10).

Then the Chronicler goes on to tell quite another story of Manasseh: "Therefore the LORD brought upon them the captains of the army of the king of Assyria, who took Manasseh with hooks, bound him with bronze *fetters*, and carried him off to Babylon" (v. 11).

Whereas the prophets had failed to convert Manasseh, the Assyrians succeeded: "Now when he was in affliction, he implored the LORD his God, and humbled himself greatly before the God of his fathers, and prayed to Him; and He received his entreaty, heard his supplication, and brought him back to Jerusalem into his kingdom. Then Manasseh knew that the LORD *was* God" (vv. 12–13). When at last he returned to Jerusalem, Manasseh was a changed man (vv. 14–17). This repentance on his part inspired a much later apocryphon called *The Prayer of Manasseh*, often included among the Odes in the Septuagint and an authorized part of the Vulgate.

This sojourn of Judah's king in Mesopotamia is also recorded in an Assyrian source called *The Prism of Esarhaddon*. According to this archival document, the new emperor, Esarhaddon (680–669), compelled the kings in the western part of the Assyrian Empire to come to the capital of Assyria to render their obeisance. The *Prism* names all these kings, among whom was *Me-na-si-i Ia-ú-di*, Manasseh of Judah.

This text is of great assistance in understanding the account in 2 Chronicles. Josephus, unfamiliar with the *Prism*, rather seriously misinterprets the biblical story by supposing it was the Babylonians who abducted Manasseh (*Antiq.* 10.3.1). This was scarcely possible, because the event antedated the rise of Babylon by several decades.

The truth is deeper and more interesting. According to *The Prism of Esarhaddon*, these subject kings were brought to Nineveh, which is exactly what we would expect, Nineveh being the capital of the Assyrian Empire. Why, then, does 2 Chronicles say "Babylon"? Surely this does not mean the city of Babylon, which would make no sense in that historical setting. "Babylon" here refers, rather, to the region of Babylon, "Babylonia," a territory then contained in the Assyrian Empire. In the much later perspective of the Chronicler, Nineveh was a place in "Babylon," much as it is now a place in Iraq.

We perceive, then, what the Chronicler has done. He has portrayed Manasseh's forced journey to Mesopotamia as a kind of small Babylonian captivity, prefiguring the great captivity of the Jews a century later. Thus the repentance of Manasseh in exile and his subsequent liturgical reforms at Jerusalem foreshadowed the repentance of the Jews, languishing in Babylon, and their subsequent restoration of worship at Jerusalem. This subtle historical analogy touches a dominant theme of the Chronicler, who regarded the orthodox worship of God as the final goal and the true significance of biblical history.

Conversion seldom carries with it the ability to set right all the harm that one has accomplished by doing evil. We see this in the case of King David, whose crimes, even after he had repented of them, continued to harm his kingdom.

Similarly, Manasseh repented and mended his ways, but the evil he had done continued to outlive him. Manasseh's devout grandson, Josiah, would be obliged to deal with the evil legacy of his repentant grandfather. Indeed, even the reforms of Josiah were unable to do more than delay the doom that would befall Jerusalem by reason of that evil legacy (34:23–28). In fact, when Jerusalem fell at last to the Babylonians in 587, "at the commandment of the LORD *this* came upon Judah, to remove *them* from His sight because of the sins of Manasseh, according to all that he had done" (2 Kings 24:3).

Most of us have noticed how wickedness, once committed, appears to take on an independent existence. However, this existence is only apparently independent, because in truth "we do not wrestle against flesh and blood, but against principalities, against powers, against the rulers of the darkness of this age, against spiritual *hosts* of wickedness in the heavenly *places*" (Eph. 6:12). Satan has his own designs on history.

Unfortunately, the son of Manasseh, Amon (642–640), followed the earlier rather than the later example of his father (vv. 21–23). The brief description of his death (vv. 24–25; 2 Kings 21:23–24) suggests a kind of palace coup, put down in turn by the populace, who installed Amon's proper heir, Josiah.

2 CHRONICLES 34

JOSIAH'S CHRONOLOGY SEEMS PRETTY WELL ESTABLISHED FOR US. Reasonably placing the beginning of his reign (under a regency, of course) in 640, we surmise he was born in 648 (v. 1), fathered by the 16-year-old Amon (cf. 33:21). Josiah himself became a father at age 16 (cf. 36:2). It was 632, and he had a serious religious conversion that same year (v. 3). Fathering children and getting serious about God often go together.

On reaching age 20 in the year 628, Josiah took the kingdom in hand and initiated a religious reform of the nation (vv. 3–7). There are five things noticeable about this reform.

First, Josiah got rid of only the Canaanite gods (vv. 3–4). Evidently the Assyrian gods had already been purged by the repentant Manasseh (33:15).

Second, in the pursuit of this reform Josiah ignored his northern border (v. 6). He could afford to do this, because the recently weakened Assyrian warrior would never again show his face at the walls of Jerusalem. The last of the great Assyrian emperors, Asshurbanipal (668–633), had lately died, and none of his feeble successors could ever again threaten the western end of the Fertile Crescent. The Assyrian Empire was already in grievous decline, and the Babylonian king, Nabopolassar (626–605), would soon be in full revolt against it. Asshur would fall to the Babylonians in 614, Nineveh in 612, Haran in 610, and the dreaded Assyria would be no more.

Third, only the Chronicler notes that the Levites were charged with the financial oversight of the refurbishing of the temple (vv. 11b–13). This is not only the kind of detail we expect in Chronicles, but it also ties the Levites to the discovery of the scroll in the temple. In the next chapter it will be obvious that the priests and Levites were very much involved in Josiah's project of reform.

Fourth, the prophet Jeremiah seconded Josiah's reform. Apparently born in 640, the very year of Josiah's succession, Jeremiah received his prophetic call in 627 (Jer. 1:2), five years before the discovery of the scroll in the temple. Thus, Jeremiah was only 18 when the scroll was discovered. Josiah's reform seems to have been something of a youth movement. In 627 Jeremiah complained, in fact, that he was still a mere boy (Jer. 1:6).

Fifth, Josiah's reform involved the refurbishing of the temple, and as preparations were being made for it in 622, a mysterious scroll was discovered there (v. 8). Except for the mention of the Levites, the Chronicler (vv. 9–11a, 14–18) describes this discovery pretty much as it is described in 2 Kings 22:3–7. The scroll is described as containing "the Law of the LORD *given* by Moses," and biblical scholars since patristic times have suspected that it was either the Book of Deuteronomy or a significant portion thereof.

On hearing the scroll read and learning its content, Josiah was horrified, realizing how woefully he and the people had failed to observe the Law (v. 19). Even his extensive reforms, which had been in progress for several years, did not measure up. The king had a sense of impending doom by reason of the nation's accumulated sins over many generations, so he sent his companions to seek prophetic guidance on the matter (vv. 20–21).

They consulted the prophetess Huldah (v. 22), who did them the kindness of telling them the worst. The accumulation of evil was already too great, she said, for Judah to evade its inevitable results. The scales were already overbalanced to the point of a relentless crash, and there was no way to stop the forces of history unleashed by so much sin. The nation would soon perish because of its chronic infidelities (vv. 23–25). Only thus, remarked Josephus, could the Lord vindicate the warnings of the prophets (*Antiq.* 10.4.2).

The sole consolation held out by Huldah was the guarantee that the punishment of the nation would not come to pass during the lifetime of the present godly king (vv. 26–28). Since Josiah was a relatively young man at the time, perhaps there were those who took comfort in the thought that they too would be spared the vision of the impending punishment. Alas, they did not know how little time Josiah had left in this world. The king would be dead in thirteen years.

Josiah took this prophecy of Huldah in the same spirit of humility that he displayed when the Law was first read to him. Resolving that whatever time was left would be spent in the pure service of God, he caused the Book of the Law to be read aloud in the presence of the national leaders and whoever else could join them (vv. 29–30). He would not spare them the bad news. He would not permit them to walk blindly into the future or put their hopes in a vain sense of security. Their days were numbered, after all, and Josiah thought it a mercy that they should know it. God was still God, and man still owed Him pure service (v. 31). Josiah would continue to love God "with all his heart and all his soul," an expression he had recently learned from reading the sacred text of Deuteronomy.

The chapter's closing verses (32–33) are proper to the Chronicler.

2 CHRONICLES 35

༄༁

ALTHOUGH 2 KINGS 23:21–23 TELLS OF THE PASSOVER observed in Jerusalem in the year the scroll was discovered, the account of that same celebration here in Chronicles is far more ample and detailed. Indeed, verses 2–18 of the present chapter are peculiar to the Chronicler.

Josiah entrusted the organization and preparation for this feast to the ever-reliable Levites, who were especially charged with the actual slaying of the paschal lambs (vv. 3–5). At each part of the ritual the Levites performed their sundry duties as assistants, musicians, and door-keepers (vv. 10–15).

So great was Josiah's celebration of Passover that the Chronicler's mind was forced back to the time of Samuel to find its equal (v. 18). For two reasons this high estimate is unexpected. First, it makes Josiah's celebration of Passover eclipse notable Passover celebrations of David, Solomon, and Hezekiah. Second, it suggests a high liturgical standard during the premonarchical period, a time about which, as we have seen, the Chronicler had fairly little to say at the beginning of the book. These considerations render the Chronicler's assessment a bit surprising.

The Chronicler is careful to note that this Passover celebration involved "all Judah and Israel" (v. 18). Josiah's ability to bring together the entire chosen people, all the descendants of those who celebrated that first Passover on the night before the Exodus, indicates the recent political changes in the Fertile Crescent. Obviously no one was any longer afraid of what the Assyrians might think.

It is very significant of Josiah's thinking, moreover, that he invited the remnants of the northern tribes to the feast, as Hezekiah had done in the previous century. The Passover was not just any feast. It was the feast in which Israel was separated from all other peoples of the earth. It was the feast that rendered Israel God's chosen people. Therefore, it was preeminently the feast of the unity of the people of God.

Being restricted to Jerusalem, Josiah's celebration of the feast, we observe, corresponded to the prescription of Deuteronomy, which we believe to have formed, at least in part, the scroll so recently discovered.

In that text it was commanded, "You may not sacrifice the Passover within any of your gates which the LORD your God gives you; but at the place where the LORD your God chooses to make His name abide, there you shall sacrifice the Passover" (Deut. 16:5–6).

Perhaps more than any other feast in the liturgical calendar, Passover roots Israel's worship in the concrete, documented facts of history. The annual feast itself is part of the historical continuity inaugurated by the events remembered on that holiest of nights. Israel represents, in this respect, a religious adherence profoundly different from that of the religions of India, which involve various efforts to escape from history into some kind of experience transcendent to history. Israel's worship does not endeavor to escape the flow of history but to place the worshippers into the people's historical identity established by historical events. Those who keep this feast become one with those who have always kept it, including those who stood to eat the Passover on that first night, protected by the sprinkled blood of the paschal lambs.

The proper celebration of the Passover, however, is more than a "then and now." The "then and now" form only the two extremes of the greater continuity. The full continuity is also important, because this feast is essentially an inherited feast, and the inheritance is received, not simply from the distant past, but from the more immediate past of the previous generation of worshippers.

What was true of Israel's celebration of the paschal feast is, of course, likewise true of that new Pascha celebrated by Christians (in the identical historical continuity, for those Israelites were our own forefathers!). This is how we should understand the words of the apostle Paul, who wrote to the Corinthians at Passover season, "Christ, our Passover, was sacrificed for us. Therefore let us keep the feast" (1 Cor. 5:7–8).

The closing verses (20–27) of this chapter bring us to the year 609, when the final remnants of the Assyrian army were destroyed at the Battle of Carchemish. Nineveh, the Assyrian capital, had fallen to the allied forces of the Medes and Babylonians three years earlier in 612 (to the great joy of the prophet Nahum, who made this the theme of his book). In 610 the vestigial refugee government of Assyria was driven out of Haran, at the top of the Fertile Crescent. The Assyrian situation had become desperate.

To Necho (610–594), the new pharaoh who took the throne of Egypt that very year, this was not a good development. Necho was certain that the Babylonians, after they finished off the Assyrians, would begin to cast their gaze down toward the southwestern border of the Fertile Crescent, the land of Egypt. Deciding, then, to cast in his lot with the remaining forces of Assyria, Necho marched his army northwards along the coastal road through the Carmel range, heading toward a rendezvous with the Assyrians at Carchemish on the Euphrates River, with the hope that with joined forces they might stop the march of the Babylonians and the Medes.

This road lay, of course, right through the territory of Judah, and King Josiah was forced to make some determination about the matter. Perhaps recalling that his great-grandfather Hezekiah had been friendly toward Babylon (32:31), and certainly remembering all that the Holy Land had suffered at the hands of the Assyrians, Josiah determined to throw in his lot with Babylon. He resolved to march counter to Pharaoh Necho and stop him from reaching Carchemish. When their two armies met at a crossroads on the plain beneath Armageddon, the "hill of Megiddo," King Josiah perished in the battle.

Whereas in 2 Kings this story is told in two-and-a-half verses (23:28–30a), the Chronicler provides a longer, more detailed, more colorful account. According to this account, Pharaoh Necho tried to dissuade Josiah from fighting him, claiming even the will, protection, and providence of God for the side of the Egyptians (v. 21). What is important here is not the nature of Necho's claim, but the fact that the Chronicler apparently agreed with it (v. 22). In the narrator's eyes, this was one more occasion when a king of Judah refused to pay heed to a message from on high, with disastrous results for the kingdom. He will summarize this theme in the next chapter (36:15–16).

2 CHRONICLES 36

ॐ

WHEREAS 2 KINGS (23:31—25:21) DEVOTES 58 VERSES to narrating the history of Judah after the death of Josiah, the Chronicler needs only a dozen verses to describe the same period (609–587 BC). It was a miserable time, easily summarized, and the Chronicler was not disposed to dwell on it.

As we have suggested, Josiah's own motives may have been mixed when he determined to attack the invading army of Pharaoh Necho. The decline of the Assyrian Empire, a process requiring two decades until its fall, had created something of a political vacuum in the western half of the Fertile Crescent. In Judah itself at least one political faction favored the rise of Babylon, and this faction apparently included Josiah himself. The books of 2 Kings and Jeremiah indicate also the emergence of another party that preferred an alliance with Egypt. One side or the other would prevail, because it was becoming evident to everyone that Judah's days of political independence were at an end.

The first part of the present chapter (vv. 1–10) illustrates the political struggles in which these competing forces worked themselves out. His eldest son Jehoiakim did not succeed Josiah at his death, because a popular uprising, apparently motivated by pro-Babylonian sympathies, gave the crown to another son, Jehoahaz/Eliakim (v. 1). Within three months, however, Pharaoh Necho intervened and took this son hostage into Egypt. To replace him on the throne of Judah he chose Josiah's older son, Jehoiakim, who was perhaps more favorable—and certainly more acceptable—to Egypt (vv. 2, 4, 5). The annual tribute Judah paid to Egypt made manifest Judah's *de facto* subjugation (v. 3).

After eleven years, nonetheless, Babylon decided to make its move on the southwest end of the Fertile Crescent, deposing Jehoiakim and replacing him with his son Jehoiachin (vv. 6–9). (In v. 9 read "eighteen" instead of "eight," following the Greek manuscripts and 2 Kings 24:8.) Within three months the Babylonians found the latter choice also unacceptable, so Jehoiachin was likewise deposed and replaced by his uncle, Zedekiah (vv. 10–11), the youngest son of Josiah. (In v. 10 Zedekiah is called Jehoiachin's "brother," but this noun is to be understood in the normal biblical sense of "kinsman." Only rarely does the word "brother" carry in Semitic languages the strict and limited sense it has in English.)

The Chronicler especially blames this Zedekiah, the last of Judah's kings, for ignoring the sound counsel of Jeremiah, the last of the pre-exilic prophets. Indeed, the entire leadership of the nation is charged here with polluting the temple (v. 14), apparently with various forms of both idolatry and neglect. This indictment, found only in the Chronicler, touches at the center of his theological interest in history.

In addition, the Chronicler speaks of two pre-exilic spoliations of the vessels of the temple by the Babylonians (only one of which is mentioned in 2 Kings 23:13). These sacred vessels of the worship thus suffer, as it were, an early captivity in Babylon. (The Book of Ezra will give much attention to their return.)

The Chronicler perceived such defilements of the temple and its worship, by both the chosen people and their enemies, as attacking the being and identity of Israel. Eviscerating the very reason for Israel's existence, these defilements led inevitably to the downfall of Jerusalem.

The Chronicler indicts the leaders of Judah for their sustained refusal to take seriously the warnings of the messengers by whom the Lord "sent *warnings* to them . . . rising up early and sending *them*" (v. 15). This quaint latter expression the Chronicler took straight out of the Book of Jeremiah, where it is common (7:13, 25; 25:3, 4; 26:5; 29:10; 35:15; 44:4; cf. 11:7; 32:33), though it appears nowhere else in Holy Scripture.

The Chronicler, even as he invokes the prophetic literature against his countrymen, appeals to the Wisdom literature by accusing them of mockery (*mal'bim*), contempt (*bozim*), and scoffing (*mitta't'im*) (v. 16). That is to say, the leaders of Judah have proved themselves to be the consummate "fools," who not only refuse to receive instruction but treat with malice those who would instruct them. Against such as these, says the Chronicler, there is no remedy.

As our reading of Chronicles would lead us to expect, Jerusalem's fall is described chiefly in terms of the temple (vv. 17, 19) and its sacred vessels (v. 18).

Judah's exile in Babylon lasted until 517 BC (v. 20), exactly seventy years from Jerusalem's fall in 587. The Chronicler notes that Jeremiah (25:12) prophesied this detail (v. 21). That number, seventy, serves in the Bible as a kind of ironic Sabbath, because during all this period it is a fact that the land lay fallow and no one worked on it.

Because there was no temple, no active priesthood nor sacrifice during the seventy years of the Babylonian Captivity, that period held no theological interest for the Chronicler. He skipped it completely and went straight to the downfall of Babylon and the return of the exiles in the Book of Ezra.

In a later editing, the Book of Chronicles was separated from Ezra and Nehemiah, all of which had originally served as a narrative sequence, and thus became the final book in the Hebrew Scriptures (split into two at the time of the Greek Septuagint, as we have seen). Hence, this last page of Chronicles became the last page of the Hebrew Bible. When this later editing was done, the opening verses of the Book of Ezra were borrowed and added to the end of Chronicles (vv. 22–23), an arrangement that permitted the sacred text to end on a positive and optimistic note. Christian editions of Holy Scripture place Chronicles in a more sensible sequence.

ABOUT THE AUTHOR

Patrick Henry Reardon is pastor of All Saints Antiochian Orthodox Church in Chicago, Illinois, and Senior Editor of *Touchstone: A Journal of Mere Christianity.*

ALSO BY PATRICK HENRY REARDON

The Trial of Job

"The Book of Job always constituted essential and formative reading about the ways of the soul. This has always been the conviction of the spiritual classics through the centuries. Yet, for some reason, the figure of Job is elusive to us—possibly because he seems so comfortably distant; or perhaps because he seems so frightfully close. What Fr. Patrick Reardon achieves with this book is to render Job comprehensible (to those of us who are still lay readers of Scripture), tangible (to those who have not yet tasted the way of darkness and despair), and accessible (to those who have already experienced any form of brokenness and broken-heartedness). Ultimately, all of us identify with one or another aspect of Job's life. As life inevitably informs and as this book intuitively confirms, one cannot sing Psalms without having read Job!"

—Fr. John Chryssavgis, Author of *Light Through Darkness* and *Soul Mending*
Paperback, 112 pages (ISBN 1-888212-72-1) Order No. 006812—$10.95*

Christ in the Psalms

A highly inspirational book of meditations on the Psalms by one of the most insightful and challenging Orthodox writers of our day. Avoiding both syrupy sentimentality and arid scholasticism, *Christ in the Psalms* takes the reader on a thought-provoking and enlightening pilgrimage through this beloved "prayer book" of the Church.

Which psalms were quoted most frequently in the New Testament, and how were they interpreted? How has the Church historically understood and used the various psalms in her liturgical life? How can we perceive the image of Christ shining through the psalms? Lively and highly devotional, thought-provoking yet warm and practical, *Christ in the Psalms* sheds a world of insight upon each psalm, and offers practical advice for how to make the Psalter a part of our daily lives.
Paperback, 328 pages (ISBN 1-888212-20-9) Order No. 004927—$17.95*

Christ in His Saints

In this sequel to *Christ in the Psalms,* popular pastor, author, and scholar Patrick Henry Reardon once again applies his keen intellect to a topic he loves most dearly. Here he examines the lives of almost one hundred and fifty saints and heroes from the Scriptures—everyone from Abigail to Zephaniah, Adam to St. John the Theologian. This well-researched work is a veritable cornucopia of Bible personalities: Old Testament saints, New Testament saints, "Repentant saints," "Zealous saints," "Saints under pressure" . . . they're all here, and their stories are both fascinating and uplifting.

But *Christ in His Saints* is far more than just a biblical who's who. These men and women represent that ancient family into which, by baptism, all believers have been incorporated. Together they compose that great "cloud of witnesses" cheering us on and inspiring us through word and deed.

Paperback, 320 pages (ISBN 1-888212-68-3) Order No. 006538—$17.95*

OTHER BOOKS OF INTEREST

First and Second Corinthians: Straight from the Heart
by Fr. Lawrence Farley

The community Paul founded in Corinth gave him both joy and grief, for he was to encounter problems there of disunity, sin, and arrogance—including a rejection by some of his own apostolic authority. His two epistles to the Corinthians came straight from the heart, as he appeals to them to live in peace, in righteousness, in generosity, and not to resist his God-given authority. His Corinthian correspondence abides as a lasting legacy and a challenge for all churches everywhere.

Paperback, 319 pages (ISBN 1-888212-53-5) Order No. 006129—$17.95*

The Gospel of Mark: The Suffering Servant
by Fr. Lawrence Farley

Israel expected the Messiah to be a conquering hero who would liberate the Jews from their Roman servitude. But instead, Christ came as a suffering servant to liberate all mankind from slavery to sin. The Gospel of Mark records Christ's public ministry as a journey to the Cross, yet—paradoxically again—as a time of vigorous action when His miracles astounded the multitudes, and His boldness infuriated His foes.

Paperback, 224 pages (ISBN 1-888212-54-3) Order No. 006035—$16.95*

Romans: A Gospel for All
by Fr. Lawrence Farley

The Apostle Paul lived within a swirl of controversy. False Christians—Judaizers—dogged his every step, slandering his motives, denying his apostolic authority, and seeking to overthrow his Gospel teaching. They argued their case loudly, and Paul knew that he must give the literary performance of his life. The result was the Epistle to the Romans, in which he demonstrates the truth of his Gospel—a Gospel for all men—and thereby vindicates his apostolic authority.

Paperback, 208 pages (ISBN 1-888212-51-9) Order No. 005675—$15.95*

The Prison Epistles:
Philippians – Ephesians – Colossians – Philemon
by Fr. Lawrence Farley

From the depths of a Roman prison, words of encouragement and instruction flowed from the tongue of the great Apostle Paul. Written down by scribes, his words went forth as a series of letters to Christian communities throughout the Roman Empire. The Apostle Paul may have been fettered and shackled to a series of Roman guards, but the Word he preached remained unfettered and free. Contains commentaries on the epistles to the Philippians, Ephesians, Colossians, and Philemon —which were written while the Apostle Paul was in prison.

Paperback, 224 pages (ISBN 1-888212-52-7) Order No. 006034—$15.95*

THE ORTHODOX STUDY BIBLE:
New Testament and Psalms

An edition of the New Testament and Psalms that offers Bible study aids written from an Orthodox perspective. Prepared under the direction of canonical Orthodox theologians and hierarchs, *The Orthodox Study Bible* presents a remarkable combination of historic theological insights and practical instruction in Christian living. *The Orthodox Study Bible* also provides a personal guide to help you apply biblical truths to your daily life with such excellent aids as: carefully prepared study notes on the text; a chart of Scripture readings to offer guidance for daily devotions; a guide for morning and evening prayers; readings for feast days; quotations from early Church Fathers such as St. John Chrysostom, St. Ignatius of Antioch, St. Gregory of Nyssa, and St. Athanasius; a glossary of Orthodox Christian terminology; and the New King James Version translation with center-column cross references and translation notes.

Genuine Leather Edition—$50.95*; Hardcover Edition—$30.95*; Paperback Edition—$24.95*

Journey to the Kingdom:
Reflections on the Sunday Gospels
by Fr. John Mack

Reflections on selected Sunday Gospel readings. Father John's insights into familiar Bible passages that we have often heard, but may not truly have understood, are excellent. He takes us through the highlights of the church year and lovingly opens up the Gospel stories to us with patristic and biblical wisdom. Many of the reflections are filled with stories of the saints, as well as observations about living in the twenty-first century that lead us to ask deeper questions about our own lives. *Journey to the Kingdom* deals with sin and grace, repentance and confession, living by faith, and many other needful topics.

Paperback, 208 pages (ISBN 1-888212-27-6) Order No. 005132—$14.95*

Sola Scriptura
by Fr. John Whiteford

An Orthodox analysis of a Protestant bastion: private interpretation of Scripture. Exposes the fallacies on which this doctrine is based and explains the Orthodox approach to Holy Scripture.

47-page staple-bound book (ISBN 1-888212-04-7) Order No. 001983—$3.95*

*Plus applicable tax and postage & handling charges.

Please call Conciliar Press at 800-967-7377 for complete ordering information, or order online at www.conciliarpress.com.